MW01028728

"Hope delayed makes the heart sick,
but a longing fulfilled is a tree of life."
Proverbs 13:12

THE SONG OF MY HOPE

HOW TO KEEP HOPE ALIVE THROUGH ADVERSITY

A TRUE STORY

BETSY KAY RIDGWAY, M.S.

Dear Jeanette,
May the God of hope
fill you!
Betsy
Ridgway

ISBN 978-1-64416-652-9 (paperback)
ISBN 978-1-64458-250-3 (hardcover)
ISBN 978-1-64416-653-6 (digital)

Christian Faith Publishing, Inc.
832 Park Avenue
Meadville, PA 16335
www.christianfaithpublishing.com

Printed in the United States of America

Praise for *The Song of My Hope*

"*The Song of My Hope* reveals how to live in a state of hopefulness despite circumstances that are beyond our control. Numerous times Betsy Kay Ridgway faced trauma and crises, yet she found hope and joy in God's abundant love. This book provides us with encouragement in facing life's struggles through her true stories of heartache and pain. Her secret lies in knowing and trusting God. I found her powerful story to be one of miraculous faith, an ordinary woman who believes in an extraordinary God."

—Julie White, M.A.
Executive Director, The Unfolding Soul
Author of *Meet Me by the Water*

"Walking with Betsy Kay Ridgway through her journey past childlessness, to the decision to adopt and then become an advocate for her special needs child, connected me to all of the emotions a mother endures for the love of her children. But she does not leave us wandering in overwhelming disappointment. She shows us the path to One who can take our hand too and walk with us through life's darkest moments. I was enriched from her book, *The Song of my Hope,* because we took the journey together."

—Dellena Ludwig
Author of *Where Did the Dinosaurs Come From?*

DEDICATION

This book is dedicated to all of you who struggle
with hopelessness, discouragement or despair.
This book was written to light your path
toward hope!

Because of our deep gratitude to
Children's Hospital of Orange County (CHOC),
as well as the Make-A-Wish Foundation,
a portion of the proceeds from this book
will be donated to both of them.
May God bless them!

CONTENTS

TOPICAL STUDY GUIDE BY CHAPTER

WITH GRATITUDE

I'm very grateful for the love and support my two sisters have given me from the very first moment we adopted our boys. Pam was videotaping the moment we first held Sean. She was at the hospital almost as much as I was when Sean was sick. I'll always be thankful for the time Arlene flew down to babysit Cameron and Sean so Russ and I could celebrate our first vacation in fifteen years. As I departed, I jokingly suggested she potty-train Sean while we were away, and she did! I will be forever appreciative of my sisters!

I have amazing friends who prayed me through so many heartbreaking difficulties over the years. They also made countless meals and helped with day-to-day challenges. My deep thanks also go to Paul Litzinger for his photographs and artistic assistance to beautify my book (www.plpics. com). God has abundantly blessed me with dear friends!

My parents, who are with the Lord, and Russ' parents on the East coast provided lots of material support over the years. Raising special needs kids is a costly adventure, and they helped support us along the way. The many delightful gifts they provided at the holiday season always cheered our spirits.

I was fortunate to be blessed with the most patient man in the world. My love for Russ reaches the heavens! I know God brought us together for the purposes of celebrating a story for His glory. My gratitude for the Lord for all He has done to bless us will forever be in my heart.

Russ, Betsy, Cameron & Sean Ridgway – 1996

INTRODUCTION

"He put a new song in my mouth,
a song of praise to our God;
many will see, have awe and will trust in the LORD."
(Psalm 40:3)

Most of my childhood dreams have come true, but not in the way I ever could have imagined. I now see how God wove some unimaginable events into the tapestry of my life and created a shimmering piece of art-work. Only the Master Planner could use my pain and trials and transform them into a blessing of beauty. How else could I explain the years of pain with a song of hope? Over the years, when my friends have asked me how I survive all of our hardships, I would answer, "The joy of the Lord is my strength" (Nehemiah 8:10). He turns my weakness into strength.

I desperately searched for love during my twenties. After turning thirty, I found my one True Love. On that day, the Lord scooped me up in His arms and has never let me go. Through every trial and time of testing, God has comforted me and guided me to dwell beside still waters. He revives me every morning by washing me in His Word. This gives me the strength to meet every new challenge year after year. By trusting Him on my journey, He has rewarded me with a deep and abiding faith. This is my story of love, loss and a new song of hope!

1

The Taste of Terror

Be strong, and let your heart take courage
all you who hope in the Lord.

—Psalm 31:24

Hearing my eight-month-old baby cry, I scurried downstairs to prepare his morning bottle. As we cuddled on the couch, nothing seemed out of the ordinary as I lifted the bottle to his lips. However, our lives would forever be changed by what happened next. As I looked down into his beautiful face, I noticed his right eye and the right side of his lips were twitching. He wasn't able to suck on his bottle. Completely alarmed, I raced up the stairs with Sean in my arms to wake my sleeping husband, Russ. He quickly called the pediatrician, who instructed us to immediately go to the emergency room. Trying to keep our panic at bay, we drove with Sean bundled in his PJs and a blanket. Once there, Russ couldn't stay long as he had to go to work. So I waited outside Sean's room in the hallway as they attempted to start an IV. They worked while he cried for ninety minutes. I was crying too. Many more tears would be shed in the years to come. My life with a critically-ill baby was just beginning.

Russ rejoined me at the hospital after his shift. We had checked in at 6:30 a.m. on a Friday morning, and now it was 7:00 p.m. They were still running tests and wouldn't finish until midnight. Russ and I were hovering over Sean's cold, metal crib when the pediatrician burst in with terrifying news. She said very bluntly, "Sean has a mass in his brain and we need to rush him to the Children's Hospital of Orange County (CHOC)."

I suddenly felt like a jellyfish out of water, and I collapsed into a chair. I was completely stunned. Russ responded, "We need to call Jerry and Maryann." Our teachers from our Adult Bible Fellowship at our church were the first ones we called at the hospital eighteen hours prior, asking for a prayer chain to be started. Like a robot, I went over to the phone and dialed their number. Maryann answered, "So what did you find out about Sean?" I opened my mouth to speak, but no words escaped. Russ came to my rescue and told Maryann the horrifying news. She said she would immediately start praying.

It was too late to call my parents and Russ' dad and stepmom lived on the East Coast. Although Russ' mom lived nearby, she was in poor health, so we delayed calling our family members. Within thirty minutes, Jerry and Maryann swooshed into our room. Seeing them brought us comfort. They hugged us and stood near. Their presence felt like a warm, cozy blanket. My thoughts were starting to clear. I relayed the doctor's report. Sean would be transferred to CHOC and be under the care of a neurosurgeon.

We hugged our teachers good-bye and thanked them for coming over in the middle of the night. They would be the hub for communicating our prayer requests to our large church family. We felt blessed to be the center of prayer coverage at a time of many unknowns. This would be the beginning of my journey to establishing my faith on a much deeper level. But for now, I was very afraid, and there were a million unknowns.

Upon our arrival to CHOC, the nursing staff was friendly and efficiently connected Sean to an IV within minutes. I recalled our ninety-minute ordeal at the other hospital with anger. Thankfully, this hospital was trained in caring for babies and children, so I felt comfort in that knowledge.

An MRI of Sean's brain was immediately taken, and shortly thereafter, the neurosurgeon was giving us the cold, hard facts. If Sean survived the surgery, he might be blind, deaf, mute, or paralyzed. I suddenly felt like I was falling off a cliff. Thankfully, we were seated when he gave us this devastating news.

The neurosurgeon displayed the brain scans for our review. He pointed out the brain tumor, highlighted in white. It was massive and irregularly-shaped. He explained that he wouldn't know what type of tumor this was until they surgically removed it on Monday. The surgery results would be news that cut like a knife right through my heart.

My "patience" muscles were getting another workout. Waiting through the infertility and adoption processes was the worst pain I had ever experienced at that time. We had waited eight-and-a-half years to become parents, and now at eight months old, Sean's life was hanging in the balance. God was preparing us for a much bigger trial.

The weekend was a blur of phone calls. No visitors were allowed yet. We made plans to stay at the Ronald McDonald House across the street. This temporary home was truly a God-send. The bedroom upstairs was cozy with a beautiful kitchen and dining room on the floor level.

Over the next month, our church friends would bring us our meals, making us feel cared for and deeply loved. For the next few months, I would feel like I was floating in a protective, heavenly cloud. The prayers of my friends and family were literally lifting us "up."

Thinking back to my childhood, I could never have imagined in my wildest dreams all the adventures I would take. God had the trip of a lifetime planned.

A LONGING FULFILLED

Describe a time when you experienced deep fear.

_____

_____

_____

_____

_____

_____

_____

_____

_____

What was your response to that experience?

_____

_____

_____

_____

_____

_____

_____

_____

_____

Find a Scripture (Supplement B) that overcomes fear.

_____

_____

_____

_____

_____

_____

_____

_____

_____

Each time you relive that memory or start to experience that fear, start verbalizing your Scripture above.

2

Clean-Shaven Love

My soul finds rest in God; my hope comes from Him.
—Psalm 62:5

Russ and Betsy's early years

I awoke to the aroma of pot roast and the sound of my mom humming as she efficiently prepared our lunch. This was her routine most Sunday mornings as we four kids readied for church. For decades, we would all sit down to a wonderful meal after church. This created a stability that grounded us in wonderful family traditions.

A love for my church was created from regular attendance, singing in the choir, and teaching Sunday school. Our little church became my extended family and deep bonds were formed. They provided a layer of devotion that helped me feel like I had a larger family.

Despite the cushion of love from my family and church friends, I was an anxious and shy child, and as an insecure young adult, I became an expert worrier! I had perfectionist tendencies while I tried to control my world around me. As a young adult, I was not grounded in my faith, and as a result, I felt restless and spiritually unfulfilled. At age twenty, I proceeded on a quest to satisfy my intense spiritual longing by studying many of the major world religions. They only took me on a journey away from God.

Without a strong faith, even minor losses left me feeling unbalanced. With a major loss, I would remain a prisoner of despair. I was twenty-five when my dad died suddenly of a heart attack. I was heartbroken and did not have a solid faith to lean on. For years, I would be stuck in a season of grieving.

By my late twenties I felt empty, aimless, and hopeless. I thought by this age, I would be married and have children. I felt like my dreams were slipping away.

By the world's standards, I was successful. I had an advanced education; I had traveled throughout Europe and had lived in several states. I had a high-paying job and I had boyfriends. Why, then, was I so miserable? I began to realize the source of my misery was me! I was living a self-centered life. I was leaning on my own strength for happiness and kept coming up short.

Looking for love while I was intensely insecure proved to be a dangerous duo. I was searching for a husband using a worldly measuring stick that involved engaging in premarital sex. I became pregnant at age twenty-seven. I was deeply ashamed. I was still attending my little church because my love for my church friends and singing ran deep in my heart. Now I was at a crossroad. Unfortunately, I chose to have an abortion. This experience was one of the most traumatic and deeply disturbing events in my life.

The experience of having a baby ripped out of my body was not only physically painful; it was emotionally and spiritually devastating. This trauma would haunt me for many years. I would eventually take a class on healing offered at my church for women who have had abortions. After completing the class, I felt healed and whole. I wanted to inspire other women to come forward and work toward their healing, so I spoke to two large groups. I'm thankful for the support that Jenni, our Women's Ministry Director, gave me during this time of healing.

One of the sad facts I learned in this healing class is that scarring can occur with resulting infertility. With time, I would come to regret this decision even more. Could the abortion be the cause of an agonizing ripple effect in my future?

When I turned thirty, I felt God gently calling me back to Him. I enjoyed listening to sermons on the radio and started craving contemporary Christian music. God was softening my heart, and I was finally ready to run back to Him. He was right there ready to welcome me! I was ready to let

God fill me with a stability I had never experienced. Within a few weeks, I decided to re-dedicate my life to Christ. I truly became born again. This decision would resurrect my drained spirit. My transformation would now begin.

I stood before the congregation and professed that Jesus Christ was the Lord of my life, and I was ready to listen to His voice and follow Him. From that moment on, I slowly started to feel flickers of love inside my aching heart. Pain began melting away. I was starting to feel alive! God had breathed His life back into me.

As a new Christian, I was already starting to experience a fuller and richer life. I was starting to feel whole and complete. All my life, I had been searching for this. I finally found that deep spiritual satisfaction when I gave my heart to Jesus. This filled that yearning and longing that I had in my heart. I was now ready to live my adventures with the Lord by my side.

I remember well one particular Sunday that would alter the course of my life. I was sitting in my usual spot in the first row of the choir loft. We were settled in for the sermon. I scanned the congregation and noticed a tall, young man seated near the back. I observed how his scraggly beard made him appear sad. I was determined to invite him to our youth group. After church, I made a beeline for him. He introduced himself, and then his Grandma Lura, who was standing next to him. She looked vaguely familiar. I cheerfully announced to him, "We have a youth meeting every Sunday night. We play volleyball and have a great time together. We'd love for you to join us!" I have to admit I was inviting him out of pity. He looked incredibly sad. It turned out he was not ready for a group like ours.

A few months later, on another Sunday, I was seated in my usual choir loft spot, waiting for the sermon to begin. I scanned the congregation and spied a tall and very handsome young man near the back of the church. As was my custom, I strolled up to him after church and introduced myself to him. "Hi! I'm Betsy and we'd love for you to come to our youth group tonight." Just as the last word left my mouth, I saw the same familiar older lady I had seen a few months prior.

The young man replied, "My name is Russ and this is my grandmother, Lura." Just then, I realized this was the same hairy-faced young man I had already introduced myself to a few months prior. I was quite embarrassed, but Russ was sweet and told me he felt special with all the attention.

Just then, his Grandma Lura spoke up, "Well I declare, if it isn't little Betsy! I used to teach you in Sunday school when you were about four years old."

This was a small world indeed! Her husband had passed on, and she hadn't been in the area for quite a while. Now she was back and invited her grandson Russ to join her at church. I was having trouble concentrating on her words. There were stars in my eyes. This good-looking chap was stealing my heart at first glance. Before long, we started dating. We dated for two years before becoming Mr. and Mrs. Ridgway in 1984.

Because I was thirty-two by the time I got married, I was eager to start a family. Becoming parents would take us on a journey akin to a roller-coaster ride. We would never have dreamed that it would end with a brand-new beginning.

A LONGING FULFILLED

Describe a time when you experienced regret or shame.

_____
_____
_____
_____
_____
_____
_____
_____
_____

What was your response to that experience?

_____
_____
_____
_____
_____
_____
_____
_____
_____

Find a Scripture that overcomes regret or shame and write it here.

_____

_____

_____

_____

_____

_____

_____

_____

_____

Each time you relive that memory or start to experience regret or shame, start verbalizing your Scripture above.

3

Babies Floating to Heaven

When anxiety was great within me,
Your comfort brought me joy.

—Psalm 94:19

Betsy, Ashley, and Jessica

During our first year of marriage, I became pregnant. Our whole family rejoiced! I was more than ready to be a mom. I had been dreaming of this moment my whole life. I immediately designed the nursery, filled the little dresser with baby clothes, and floated through each day, feeling dreamy and optimistic.

In my second month, I started feeling sharp twinges of pain. Sadly, within a few days, I experienced a miscarriage, which left me dizzy with questions. I just couldn't understand what went wrong. Russ and I decided to wait about a year before trying again. I needed time to emotionally heal.

Within a year, I was elated to announce to my family and friends that I was pregnant again. I felt confident that God was going to bless us with a baby. At this same time, I was trying to finish my master's degree in counseling. I was also working in an engineering company as the receptionist and technical typist. I knew that once I had my baby, I would become a full-time homemaker. I was looking forward to this new season. Unfortunately, like last time, I miscarried. This time I was angry.

I decided to turn my anger and frustration into action by having all the necessary tests to determine if there was something wrong with either Russ or me. The tests were time-consuming and painful; however, it was determined that nothing was wrong with either one of us. With this new information, we decided to try again.

After learning I was pregnant for the third time, I was not feeling elated like before. I was nervous and afraid. I told Russ I didn't even want to announce the pregnancy except to family and a few close friends. I wanted to wait until I passed the first trimester. Miscarriages usually happen within the first three months, so we waited. A week into my second trimester, I was ready to announce my pregnancy to the world again. How ironic that a week later, I would miscarry for the third time.

This time, I was devastated. I started to question God. I couldn't understand why He would let me go through one trial after another. I felt discouraged and depressed.

Depression comes when you have no hope. I hadn't learned enough Scripture yet to be familiar with this one from Romans 15:13, "May the God of hope fill you with all joy and peace as you trust in Him, so that you may overflow with hope by the power of the Holy Spirit."

Russ and I decided it was time to purchase our first home in 1987. We couldn't afford to buy a home in the beach town we grew up in, so we bought a town home about one hour away. Moving away from my hometown and church family only added to my season of sadness.

After unpacking and organizing our first home, we immediately started searching for a new church. Within a few months, we found our new church home, and started getting acquainted with the members. We had left our little church of one hundred people. We were in culture shock when our new adult Bible fellowship was this same size. The larger church had over two thousand members.

It wouldn't take long for us to feel like we were at home with our new church because of the friendly people. Suzanne was the first one to greet us and make us feel welcome. She invited us into her home, and she made us feel like a part of the family right away.

Russ and I felt like our lives were getting back on track. We were starting to feel comfortable in our new town home and our church. Making connections is essential to happiness. We were starting to feel a sense of belonging. Now I had friends I could talk to regarding my most pressing prayer request—becoming a mom.

Along my journey to motherhood, as I learned to put my hope in God, He would be teaching me about faith. God was slowly building my "faith" muscles for my future journey. I was learning to trust God to take care of all my needs.

During my waiting season, God brought a very special family into my life that would help ease my pain and bring great joy and delight. Debbie was my new neighbor. Her girls, Jessica, aged three, and Ashley, aged eighteen months, were as cute as cherubs. I frequently called Debbie to see if I could babysit. She needed relief as a single mom, and I needed to be around babies. It was a match made in heaven!

I will always remember this season of friendship with fondness. The girls referred to me as "Aunt Betsy" and I was eager to fill that role as I waited to mother my own children. Years later, as the girls reached their teen years, they would be babysitting for me. Life would come full circle. Seeds of friendship sprout in the most amazing ways!

After much prayer, Russ and I decided to try and become pregnant one more time. If God didn't bless us with a baby, we would pursue adoption. After trying for over a year with no success, Russ and I decided to start pursuing adoption anyway. Shortly after attending the adoption seminar, I learned that I was pregnant. I was still adamant about pursuing adoption if I miscarried again. In fact, I wanted us to permanently "close the door" to becoming pregnant if I miscarried again. I didn't ever want to experience that pain again. Each time, it took me about a year to recover from the emotional pain, so I felt I could only bear it one more time. Because I wasn't deeply grounded in my faith, I was still very anxious and insecure.

I was cautiously happy with this pregnancy. I was afraid to feel joy with all my heart, like I had before. After a month into the pregnancy, I decided to go on bed rest, just to assure myself that I took every precaution to maintain this pregnancy. My new church friends were very supportive and brought me meals.

Again though, this baby was not meant to be. I would need a D&C at the hospital. Although I had made it again through the first trimester, the doctor could find no reason for my miscarriage.

This was my most painful miscarriage because I knew we were shutting the door forever on having our own children naturally. I would never know the joy of looking into the sweet face of my child and saying, "You look just like your father!" This was a time of deep grieving for both Russ and me. The next month, as planned, we medically "closed the doors." The pathway to childbearing would never be open again.

I had many questions with no answers. However, I have since learned that we don't always see the big picture. God sees from the beginning to the end. His wisdom far exceeds ours. Isaiah 55:8–9 says, "For My thoughts are not your thoughts, neither are your ways My ways," declares the Lord. "As the heavens are higher than the earth, so are My ways higher than your ways and My thoughts than your thoughts."

Here we were with a trust issue. Russ and I were perfectly healthy in every way, and yet the door closed on us having our own children naturally. We would simply have to trust God to take care of us. He would provide for us in due season. It is never on our timetable, but on God's! We would be tested in this area next.

SONG OF DELIVERANCE

A poem dedicated to my five babies, once lost, now found.

Tangled web of losses, shrouded in pain and heartache.
Five of my babies floating through time,
now cuddled in the arms of Timeless Love.
His gaze turns to me, His love glows with light,
revealing the beauty of my personal tapestry.
The dark, tangled threads were all I could see
before He revealed this beautiful majesty!
The purest of gold, spun together with splendor,
a harmony of rainbows shimmering with delight.
He now sets this garment of praise on my shoulders,
and proclaims His love for me!
He quiets my pain with rivers of peace,
as He rejoices over me with deep, melodious singing,
restoring and renewing my soul.

To bestow on them a crown of beauty instead of ashes, the oil of joy instead of mourning, and a garment of praise instead of a spirit of despair. They will be called oaks of righteousness, a planting of the LORD for the display of His splendor. (Is 61:3)

The Lord your God is with you, He is mighty to save. He will take great delight in you, He will quiet you with His love, He will rejoice over you with singing. (Zeph. 3:17)

A LONGING FULFILLED

Describe a time when you experienced deep disappointment.

_____

_____

_____

_____

_____

_____

_____

_____

_____

What was your response to that experience?

_____

_____

_____

_____

_____

_____

_____

_____

_____

Find a Scripture that overcomes disappointment and write it here.

_____

_____

_____

_____

_____

_____

_____

_____

_____

Each time you relive that memory or start to experience disappointment, start verbalizing your Scripture above.

4

Parents by Any Means

*Now faith is bring sure of what we hope for,
and certain of what we do not see.*

—Hebrews 11:1

Proud dad, Russ, holding Sean

The year I turned thirty-eight was the year we pursued adoption. We shyly walked into the adoption agency on January 2, 1990, filled with fear, but the counselors put us at ease. They also gave us a million forms to fill out. We had to bear our souls on the adoption paperwork. We needed to go to the police station to be finger-printed and would end up paying a large sum of money to the adoption agency. We were working so hard to become parents. At this point, I was starting to feel resentment. All our friends were effortlessly having one baby after another.

Special occasions and holidays became unbearable. I finally stopped going to baby showers; they were just too painful. My friends were very understanding, yet this was a very lonely time in my journey. I didn't know anyone traveling the road of infertility. Also, each childless Christmas that came and went became harder and harder. I finally asked God to heal my heart so that I could truly celebrate the birth of Jesus with joy.

I was nearing my fortieth birthday in 1991. During this year, three significant events occurred. First, I became extremely ill again with ulcerative colitis. I had been diagnosed at age seventeen. I had been in and out of hospitals and had tried every medication possible. Surgery was looming as my only alternative. In July of 1991, one and a half years after we had begun the adoption process, I was advised to have a colectomy. My entire large intestine needed to be removed to rid me of this painful and debilitating disease. The doctor had told me I would need one and a half years to totally heal. I was afraid that the agency would call us while I was in the healing process, but my fear lessened as I learned how to lean on God and trust Him.

A couple of months after my surgery, I kept waking up in the middle of the night. I felt God calling me to spend time with Him, but I was stubborn! I didn't want to get out of my warm bed, even though I was having trouble falling back asleep. This routine went on for a few more nights until

I said to God, "All right, Lord, I will get up!" Although I had learned the Bible basics for the past few years, I had not developed a personal relationship with Jesus. I had no clue where to start.

I knew step one was getting out of bed, so I put on my robe and slippers and padded downstairs. I plopped myself down at the dining room table. I randomly opened my Bible and it rested open at the Psalms. My eyes were drawn to start reading this Scripture:

> Oh God, You are my God, earnestly I seek You; my soul thirsts for You in a dry and weary land where there is no water. I have seen You in the sanctuary and beheld Your power and Your glory. Because Your love is better than life, my lips will glorify You. I will praise You as long as I live, and in Your name I will lift up my hands. I will be fully satisfied as with the richest of foods; with singing lips my mouth will praise You. On my bed I remember You; I think of You through the watches of the night. Because You are my help, I sing in the shadow of Your wings. I cling to You; Your right hand upholds me. (Ps 63:1–8)

I was crying by the time I was done reading this. These eight verses changed my life. God was describing my life prior to coming down the stairs. I had been earnestly seeking Him for many years and had found Him at age thirty. It would take until this moment to know Him personally, and

He was letting me boldly know that He knew me personally. He wanted to be my protector, and the One I would run to when in need. Oh, how rich! This would be the first encounter, and eventually, I would learn to seek Him daily. After thirty years, I am still running to Him each morning to spend time reading Scriptures or listening to sermons.

The second significant event that happened that year included the death of Russ' only brother. Although Russ wasn't very close to his brother, he still experienced a tremendous amount of grieving. We all did. I was having a hard time finding joy that year, but my faith and hope were in the Lord, and I knew life was going to get better.

Although the third significant event actually occurred the same year I turned forty, it didn't materialize until later the next year. When we started the adoption process, I had prayed for God to give me a sign if I was not going to become a mom. After much prayer, I felt the Lord telling me that if I did not have a baby by the age of forty, I was not meant to be a mom. If that occurred, then God would also take away my strong desire to be a mom. I felt like I was holding my breath during my fortieth year. When my forty-first birthday came in October, there was still no baby. I felt almost as devastated as when I experienced my last miscarriage. Could God really be closing this door forever?

My confusion transformed into trust as I realized that I still had a fierce longing to be a mom. God had promised to take away this desire if I was not meant to be a mom. So I kept holding on and trusting with all my might even as I celebrated my forty-first birthday that October.

Christmas arrived and I experienced total joy for the first time in many years. I was healed! I did not feel sad or depressed that we didn't have a baby yet. I still desperately wanted a baby, but I could finally rejoice at Christmas time!

December 30, 1992, was very significant. I had now passed my year-and-a-half period of healing from my surgery. We had waited three years in the adoption process, and we were more than ready!

I never dreamed this next conversation would change the course of our lives as Russ picked up the ringing phone. We were shocked to discover it was the adoption agency. They had a twelve-day-old baby boy for us if we wanted him. The biological parents had picked Russ and me out of many other couples. They had chosen us!

There were some medical issues that caused us concern. We talked them over with a doctor, a nurse, and our families. The baby might have future challenges, but he was healthy now. Then we all prayed and prayed. By the next morning, we knew this baby was meant for us!

My sister, Pam, came with us for support as we picked up our little baby Sean from the adoption agency the next afternoon. Most couples have nine months to prepare for their baby. Although we had over eight years, becoming parents in less than twenty-four hours shocked us. We had a crib, bottles, diapers, and formula, but we were not emotionally prepared!

Thinking back to the timing of my "motherhood" prayer, I saw how God helped my faith grow. I had asked God to bless us a baby by the time I turned forty or else take away my motherhood desires. Sean was conceived during my fortieth year, even though we didn't receive him until I was forty-one. God did answer my prayer; I just needed the faith to trust Him!

A LONGING FULFILLED

Describe a time when you had difficulty trusting God.

_____

_____

_____

_____

_____

_____

_____

_____

_____

What was your response to that experience?

_____

_____

_____

_____

_____

_____

_____

_____

_____

Find a Scripture that address trust and write it here.

_____

_____

_____

_____

_____

_____

_____

_____

_____

Each time you relive that memory or start to experience distrust, start verbalizing your Scripture above.

5

Visions of Abraham

Whoever dwells in the shelter of the Most High will rest in the shadow of the Almighty. I will say of the LORD, "He is my refuge and my fortress, my God, in Whom I trust."
—Psalm 91:1–2

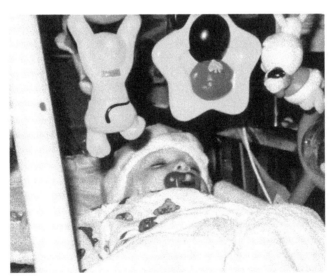

Sean, just hours after first surgery

Sean bounced into our lives on New Year's Eve. We had such celebrations! With all the usual festivities that occur when having a new baby, we were overjoyed to be blessed four times with baby showers.

After waiting for over eight years, it seems like we should have been prepared. And we were, mostly. But the shock of becoming parents in less than twenty-four hours was a bit overwhelming. I had been babysitting since junior high. I had taught Sunday school for years to children. Yet I felt like I didn't know a thing. Over the weeks, we would slowly begin to accept our new, wonderful reality.

We also had the responsibility to stay connected to the biological family. We met the parents and extended family when Sean was six weeks old. This turned out to be a historical meeting.

Sean's biological parents were there, as well as Cameron, his half brother, who was nineteen months old. We took oodles of pictures, including one of Cameron holding Sean. Little did we know that these photos would become extremely significant. We would continue to visit the family at the adoption agency, and eventually, at each other's homes, creating an open adoption.

In the first eight months of Sean's life, we had the challenges of discovering that he had severe eczema, formula allergies (he spit up every bottle), and feet that needed corrective shoes twenty-three hours a day. Sean did not sleep through the night until five months. I remember one night collapsing in the rocking chair, crying next to his crib after his night feeding. I was physically and emotionally exhausted. Special powders in his bath, special creams on his skin, changing outfits five times a day, and trying to lace up those high-top shoes with wiggling little feet just about did me in. Little did I know, but my "spiritual" muscles were getting toned for the biggest battle I was about to enter.

These challenges melted away as the pediatrician told us over the phone to rush Sean to the ER due to his facial twitches. After eighteen hours of tests and the horrible realization that Sean had a mass in his brain, we were now driving behind a speeding ambulance toward Children's Hospital of Orange County (CHOC).

Friday melted into Monday. Finally, the long weekend of waiting to speak to the neurosurgeon was over. We sat in a conference room, just the three of us. He had Sean's brain scans displayed. Even if they removed the entire tumor successfully, we might never have our whole Sean back again.

We were devastated by this news, but we clung to our faith like never before. By the time Sean began his surgery, he had hundreds of people praying for him. Before our medical journey would end, there would be thousands.

After the eight-hour surgery was over, the neurosurgeon announced that he removed the majority of the brain tumor. We then fearfully waited overnight to see if our little Sean would be coming back to us as we left him.

The next morning as we stood over his crib watching for signs of movement, we saw Sean move a finger. I cried with elation! Over the next several hours, Sean would slowly recover. Although the right side of his body was affected and his right peripheral vision was gone in both eyes, he was nearly the same. We felt this was our first miracle.

Our next miracle would concern my faith. A few days after Sean's surgery, the doctor revealed that Sean had a brain tumor called a glioblastoma multiforme, grade IV. This was an adult tumor and children hardly ever suffered from it. They had no statistics on a baby ever having one.

Sean's tumor, being grade IV, was extremely cancerous, having the capacity to double in size every seven to ten days. The six children who had this tumor in the past ten years had all died. They informed us that Sean had a 2 percent chance to live until his second birthday. We hadn't even had a chance to celebrate his first.

The oncologist recommended five months of chemotherapy, August through December. With the frequency of our trips and the distance driving to the hospital, Russ and I were grateful for our stay at the Ronald McDonald House located across the street. Once Sean fell asleep at night, I walked over to the Ronald McDonald House to sleep while Russ worked the graveyard shift. I remember being very angry at God the first few weeks. Alone at night, I begged and pleaded with the Lord. I "wrestled" with God every night while I prayed. I just couldn't believe God would take our Sean away after we suffered eight-and-a-half years trying to become parents. I kept telling God that He had no right to take him! God had given us Sean, and he was ours to keep!

One particular night of prayer forever deepened my faith. After weeks of fighting with God, I felt drained and broken. So I listened. I asked God to give me direction.

Suddenly, in my mind's eye, I saw Abraham from the Bible. Now Abraham and Sarah had waited many years to have children. In fact, they waited so long for God to bless them with a child that Sarah laughed out loud at the absurdity. Sarah was about ninety years old and Abraham was one hundred when Isaac was born. "All right, God," I thought to myself, "I could relate to this story, being an older mom!"

When Isaac was a boy, God instructed Abraham to take him up to the top of Mount Mariah and sacrifice him. Abraham had such a strong faith that he knew even if he killed his young son, God would raise him up. So with the knife poised and ready, Abraham suddenly heard a ram cry. Then God told Abraham to go sacrifice the ram instead of his beloved son.

After that scene from the Bible caught my attention, I instantly knew in my spirit that I needed to trust God, no matter what the outcome. I knew God would take care of us, even if it meant He needed to take Sean home to heaven. On that night, my faith was laid firm upon a sure foundation. I had a hope for our future. Although my trust would continue to be tested throughout Sean's illness, I had a newfound confidence in God that gave me daily peace and joy. A new courage was being born out of my suffering.

A Longing Fulfilled

Describe a time when you experienced a lack of faith.

_____

_____

_____

_____

_____

_____

_____

_____

_____

What was your response to that experience?

_____

_____

_____

_____

_____

_____

_____

_____

_____

Find a Scripture that builds up your faith.

_____

_____

_____

_____

_____

_____

_____

_____

_____

Each time you relive that memory or start to experience a lack of faith, start verbalizing your Scripture above.

6

Curious Courage

Be strong and courageous. Do not be afraid or terrified because of them, for the LORD your God goes with you; He will never leave you nor forsake you.
—Deuteronomy 31:6–8

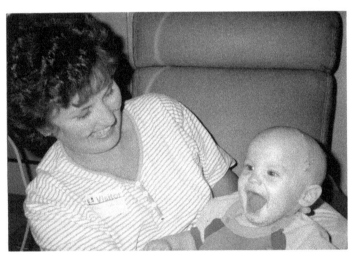

My sister, Pam, with a happy Sean after surgery

With a renewed spirit, I felt ready to face the battle for Sean's life. Friends told me they admired my courage. I would tell them I still had fear, but still needed to go about the business at hand. That's what makes courage curious. On the outside, it looks as though the courageous have complete confidence. Yet when you question these brave ones, they almost always say they were afraid while doing what needed to be done. Although I wasn't assured of Sean's outcome, I knew for certain that the Lord would protect Russ and me. That's what gave me my courage and strength.

For the rest of this year, Sean would go on to endure five months of chemotherapy, regular MRIs with general anesthesia and many procedures along the way. One of the more unpleasant tests included removing some of Sean's bone marrow from his spine to retrieve his stem cells. He was the first baby to experience this procedure where they would "wash" and store it for a future infusion date.

Hospital life had its own language and culture. Sean was cooped up in a metal crib, and I was thankful that he hadn't learned to crawl yet. Being hooked up to an IV made him somewhat of a prisoner. As his parents, the nurses taught us how to connect an IV to his broviac that was implanted into his chest. This would act as a direct line to his heart and would make administering the chemo easier. We also learned how to clean his broviac and draw his blood. I never imagined in my wildest dreams that I would be acting as Sean's nurse. Nothing is impossible with God!

We made Sean's hospital room a refuge by playing Christian lullabies and songs. Our favorite nurse, Tammy, always wanted to linger in our room. The presence of peace was there. This made up for the fact that his room was not a very stimulating environment for Sean to be growing up in. Again, I needed to trust God in this area too.

One month after Sean was admitted to CHOC, Russ and I requested to have some of the church elders come and pray for him and anoint him with oil. We were relying on the words from James 4:14–15 that says, "Is any one of you sick? He should call the elders of the church to pray over him and anoint him with oil in the name of the Lord. And the prayer offered in faith will make the sick person well." Although we had never done anything like this before, Russ and I knew this was a strong direction from the Lord.

Our church family was very sensitive to the fact that we would need help in caring for Sean during the many months ahead. Sylvia, the head of the children's department at church, signed up people from our class to come and stay with Sean so I could take regular breaks. I also remember my long-time friends, Caren, Nancy, and Cindy, coming to take me to the nearby mall for some refreshment. One would stay with Sean while the other two would get me out of the hospital setting. I was deeply appreciative of all the hours of sacrifice from my friends and church family. My sister, Pam, was by my side for the entire eight months we were in the hospital. She was amazing!

Because this time was incredibly stressful, I spent more time reading my Bible. The more time I spent with the Lord, the more He whispered in my ear and gave me direction or comfort. I was being built up as a woman of courage.

A Longing Fulfilled

Describe a time when you experienced a lack of courage.

_____

_____

_____

_____

_____

_____

_____

_____

_____

What was your response to that experience?

_____

_____

_____

_____

_____

_____

_____

_____

_____

Find a Scripture that builds up your courage and write it here.

_____

_____

_____

_____

_____

_____

_____

_____

_____

Each time you relive that memory or start to experience a lack of faith, start verbalizing your Scripture above.

7

Hovering Angels

For You make me glad by Your deeds, LORD, I
sing for joy at what Your hands have done.
                                        —Psalm 94:4

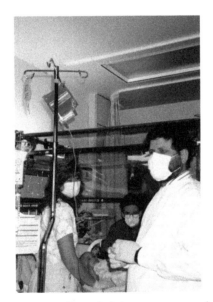

Sean, being injected with his own treated stem cells
in the oncology intensive care unit at CHOC, January 1994

An MRI taken December 1993, after four months
of chemotherapy, showed that Sean's brain tumor
had been growing again. Unusual fluid retention in

his brain became his secondary problem. Sean's neurosurgeon felt that a second surgery was useless since this brain tumor always returned. He tried to convince us to enjoy the last few months of Sean's life and accept his impending death. Deep in my spirit, I knew we still needed to fight for his life.

We prayerfully decided to pursue a second opinion and headed to Children's Hospital of Los Angeles. Sitting in a conference room, our new neurosurgeon showed us the ever-growing tumor on the x-rays. It devastated us to see it in black-and-white; the reality of it hit us squarely in the face. The doctor consented to performing the surgery, but repeated the same probability as the first surgery: blindness, inability to speak, hear, or walk. As horrific as this prospect was, we knew we needed to proceed to give Sean a chance at life.

A few days later, we were all checked in to the Los Angeles Ronald McDonald House. We nervously walked across the street to Children's Hospital and met with the surgeon. Suddenly, it was time to say good-bye before releasing Sean to the neurosurgeon for his last surgery. It was so difficult to say good-bye to our little baby again, knowing he may die, or return to us completely crippled. God was stretching us once again, and asking us to trust Him.

A couple of very dear friends were there to keep us company and keep us distracted during this surgery. They made sure to keep the conversation going during the hours of waiting. My friend Caren brought sandwiches and drinks. She brought way more than just refreshment for our bodies; this was nourishment for our sagging spirits.

Hours later, the second surgery was finally over and the neurosurgeon announced that he removed as much of the tumor as possible. Like the first surgery, he left about 10 percent of the tumor behind as he felt he might have permanently damaged Sean. I was so disappointed that the surgeon had not removed the entire tumor. It had the capacity to double in size every seven to ten days. This was one of the most aggressive tumors ever. But as in the past surgery, our most important focus was now on his recovery. An hour later, he was moving both arms and legs, and Russ and I danced around his crib! For this moment, we could rejoice!

The doctor released Sean from the hospital two and a half days later. Ironically, it was New Year's Eve, 1993. Exactly one year prior, we were picking him up from the adoption agency to begin our new life as parents. Now we were taking him home, praying we would remain parents.

The next morning, Sean starting having facial seizures, so we headed back to the children's hospital nearer our home. As soon as Sean was examined, they admitted him. He now had a high fever, and a staph infection. There was only one medication that could eradicate this infection. His life was hanging by a thread again, but I turned to God for comfort and received peace. Sean was released a few days later.

The next phase of treatment occurred one month later when he was strong enough to endure six days of high-dose chemotherapy. This was followed by a bone-marrow rescue. This was his own "washed" bone marrow being injected back into him to help kick-start his immune system. With this high-dose chemo, the doctors were hoping to kill the remaining tumor. This chemo would completely wipe out Sean's immune system. The slightest infection could kill him, so he had to now reside in the oncology intensive care unit (OICU).

We were restricted to exposing Sean to five people during this next three-month ordeal. We asked my sister, Pam, our friend Robert, and our friend Valerie to help Russ and me. Between the five of us, we would be his only outside visitors. Before entering Sean's room, we washed our hands for three very long minutes. Once inside his room, we wore a mask. The hand washing was an inconvenience, but the mask was unbearable. I felt so claustrophobic! I was learning to have more patience.

God also provided an intense blessing that I will never forget, even to this day, decades later. Although this next event happened during the day, it seemed to occur more at night. Sean would frequently look all around at the ceiling. Because I was ridiculously afraid of spiders, I would look up, expecting to see my fear become reality. This was a pretty silly notion because they cleaned Sean's room daily, including the walls and the ceiling. I wondered what Sean was seeing.

One night after Sean fell asleep, I was chatting with one of his nurses. I tentatively asked her, "Have you noticed Sean looking at the ceiling a lot?"

She immediately replied, "Yes. I think he is seeing angels!"

Although her answer stunned me, I excitedly added, "That's exactly what I was thinking!" It really shouldn't surprise us since our Christian faith talks about angels throughout the Bible. Until this point, I had not heard any stories from others about modern-day angel sightings. In the years to come, I would read many accounts of eye-witness stories about angels. Although Sean's staring startled me, it filled me with hope!

I never forgot about the possibility that Sean was seeing angels when he had cancer. A few years later, when Sean learned how to talk, I decided to see what he could tell me.

As I was tucking Sean into bed at age three and a half, I asked him, "Have you ever seen an angel?" We had never taught him about angels and he hadn't had the opportunity to be in Sunday school because of his fragile immune system.

So his answer startled me. "Oh, yes, Mommy. I've seen angels!"

Then my curiosity started overflowing as I asked, "What do they look like?" He enthusiastically replied, "They're shiny, and look like rainbows! They're in my bedroom right now and right outside the wall." I fearfully turned my head and surveyed his room and disappointedly saw nothing. In my heart though, I knew without a doubt that Sean had been surrounded by angels all during his cancer journey and was still experiencing their presence.

When you have the pure faith of a child, you are richly rewarded. The Bible talks about this in Matthew 18:2–4, "Jesus called a little child to Him, and placed the child among them. And He said, 'Truly I tell you, unless you change and become like little children, you will never enter the kingdom of heaven. Therefore, whoever takes the lowly position of this child is the greatest in the kingdom of heaven." Children accept and believe with ease. They are humble. They love to follow and please. These are the traits that Jesus loves.

While Sean received his high-dose chemo in OICU, we were warned that the side effects might bring mouth sores and extreme diaper rash. The nurses also predicted he would need to be in the OICU for at least three months.

However, God was already working miracles in Sean. He had no mouth sores and only developed a mild diaper rash. He was strong enough to go home after five-and-a-half weeks. God had Sean on the fast track for healing. We were so relieved to be able to take Sean home. Although we would be his nurses for many more months to come, we were ready for this task. We were now ready to move back home with Sean.

A Longing Fulfilled

Describe a time when you experienced hopelessness.

_____
_____
_____
_____
_____
_____
_____
_____
_____

What was your response to that experience?

_____
_____
_____
_____
_____
_____
_____
_____
_____

Find a Scripture that overcomes hopelessness and write it here.

_____

_____

_____

_____

_____

_____

_____

_____

_____

Each time you relive that memory or start to experience hopelessness, start verbalizing your Scripture above.

8

Miracles from Home, Sweet Home!

*"For I know the plans I have for you," declares
the LORD, "plans to prosper you and not to harm
you, plans to give you a hope and a future."*
                                                    —Jeremiah 29:11

Sean, content at home despite the circumstances

After settling Sean in at home, we started to feel peaceful. The noise and constant movement of the hospital had worn us to the bone. From March until December 1994, everyone entering our home had to wear a mask to protect Sean from infections. He now had no immune system, and even his immunizations would need to be given again as though he was a newborn. Russ, my sister Pam, my friends Robert and Valerie, and I were the only ones who did not need to wear a mask. For these ten months, Sean was not able to leave our home except for regular MRIs to keep a check on his brain.

Shortly after we took Sean home, our minister's wife, Judy, asked if she and two other ladies could come pray with me. Judy radiated the love of Jesus; you just wanted to be near her.

Judy, Bobbie, and Bonnie arrived the next morning, and we sat together on my couch. These were three faith-filled women, and I felt so blessed that they gave from their hearts. They boldly prayed for Sean's healing. I'll never forget that day. At that time, I had no idea that they had prepared for this time of prayer with three days of fasting. Judy would tell me about the fasting at a future time. My three friends heard a promise, and they prayed with boldness!

Sean's April 1994 MRI revealed that his tumor was completely gone! The doctors were stunned as was everyone else! Sean had been diagnosed with such a deadly brain tumor that they only gave him a 2 percent chance to live. That is a virtual death sentence. I remember Nurse Julene telling us at the beginning of Sean's cancer journey, "Somebody has to be in that 2 percent category!" I clung to this hope from that moment on!

Our God of the impossible healed our baby and our thankfulness reached the heavens! He gave us a miracle! There is always a reason to hope!

Although we were walking on clouds with the good news, we still had a lot of nursing details to take care of with Sean at home. Because we were in a tri-level town home, the stairs made us prisoners of Sean's upstairs bedroom. Being hooked up to the IV fourteen hours a day made it difficult to leave his room.

Those few hours per day of freedom were surreal. We took Sean down to the living room to encourage him to walk. He had just learned to crawl in January at thirteen months. Once he was finally off the liquid nutrition fed through an IV, we were able to encourage Sean to increase all his fine and gross motor skills. We had a therapist that visited the home to help him as well.

In June, Sean took his first steps and we cried with joy! He was eighteen months old. With his brain injury, each new milestone was a miracle. For the first time, I felt like we were living a somewhat "normal" life, just enjoying our little toddler.

In November, we finalized Sean's adoption in a unique way. Adoptions are normally held in a courtroom with a judge. Since Sean could not be out in public, a judge came to our home to legalize a beautiful adoption ceremony with friends and family. During the ceremony, I read a touching poem by Betsy Hernandez called "Here in My Heart" (1991). It describes how our child will one day grow up, but we will always have the precious memories of their childhood. This poem was bittersweet for me because we didn't know if Sean was going to grow up.

In December, Sean was doing so well that the doctors decided to remove his broviac. Russ and I were so relieved!

No more drawing blood and daily cleaning of this device. Now we could truly enjoy a more normal life.

We celebrated Sean's second birthday and Christmas on the same day so my parents, who lived quite a distance, could enjoy both. After celebrating his birthday, I quickly changed him into his Christmas outfit. We were cramming as much life as possible into one day. We never knew what tomorrow might bring. Although we had a hope for Sean to live a long life, the Lord was teaching us to value each and every minute, day by day.

A LONGING FULFILLED

Describe a time when you felt lost.

_____

_____

_____

_____

_____

_____

_____

_____

_____

What was your response to that experience?

_____

_____

_____

_____

_____

_____

_____

_____

_____

Find a Scripture that overcomes being lost and write it here.

_____

_____

_____

_____

_____

_____

_____

_____

_____

Each time you relive that memory or start to experience feeling lost, start verbalizing your Scripture above.

9

And Boovoo Makes Two

I will praise the LORD, who counsels me;
even at night my heart instructs me.

—Psalm 16:7

Betsy, Sean, and Cameron all ready for
sister-in-law, Lesley's, wedding in Maryland

With the Christmas season behind us, we
breathed a huge sigh of relief. We had just
endured seventeen months of extreme heart-

ache and fatigue. We strongly desired to live a "normal" life. I was so grateful for the smallest things. We still had to guard Sean's fragile immune system. When I took him to the grocery store or the craft store, I felt immense gratitude and joy to experience the simple pleasures of life.

We were home and relaxing after our errands when the phone rang. Like the phone call from the adoption agency two years prior, this call would also change our future.

Sean's biological grandma was calling to tell us that the birth mother was no longer capable of raising Cameron, Sean's older half brother. The grandma wanted to know if we would consider adopting Cameron. He was three and a half years old.

I sat down stunned. After the traumatic experience of parenting a critically-ill baby, I had no desire for another baby. I had been praying about adopting a preschooler one day, but not quite yet. My thought was to wait about two years so we could truly enjoy Sean's early years. Now we were at a crossroad.

In mid-January 1995, Russ and I decided to let Cameron spend weekends with us to see if he would be comfortable in our family and to see if we had the strength to dive into more responsibility. We decided to keep an open mind and gradually increase Cameron's visitations. He was confused about coming to our home, so we explained that we wanted him to get to know his half brother, which was true.

On May 15, we had an appointment with the adoption agency. They were helping us navigate the visitations with the birth family. We both had Cameron living with us on a part-time basis. We thought this day's appointment was going to entail increasing his visitation frequency. Instead, we were hit with a bombshell.

The social worker, Robin, explained to Russ and me that the birth mom had signed the release papers for Cameron. That meant we needed to decide on the spot if we were ready to adopt him, otherwise, he would go into the foster care system. What a dilemma! We weren't completely ready, but we wanted the boys to be raised together.

Robin then took me into a room by myself and asked me, "If you can't adopt Cameron, will your marriage be over?" I reluctantly answered that our marriage was on firm ground, but adopting Cameron now would put stress on it.

Robin then took Russ into a private room and asked him, "If you adopt Cameron today, will your marriage be over?"

Although he was shocked by the question, he answered a similar response, "No, but it will strain it."

It seemed to be an impossible situation; however, we both agreed that we did not want Cameron to go into foster care. We chose to adopt Cameron that very day. We signed the legal papers, and on that day, Cameron became an official Ridgway. It's rather ironic that we adopted both boys with less than twenty-four hours' notice!

May 15 was also Cameron's fourth birthday. That made the day extra sweet! As we all grew to love each other, Cameron started calling us Mom and Dad. I felt so blessed being able to raise the two boys as real brothers. Russ was also happy for that reason, but trouble was brewing.

That spring Russ' mom's health continued to deteriorate, and we had to admit her to a convalescent home. Thankfully, Russ' Aunt Kathy took care of all the details.

We were now in survival mode. Sean and Cameron fought constantly. It's rather ironic that both boys were used to being an only child, but I had a feeling it was more than sibling rivalry.

We thought Sean's aggression was due to his speech delays. He tried to pronounce "Cameron," but it started out as "Mammin," then "Cammin" and finally "Boovoo" for brother. Eventually, it would turn into "Brudder." His speech would bring us a chuckle, but his aggression was very troubling.

I finally decided to take Sean to a neurologist. At age three, he was diagnosed with attention deficit hyperactivity disorder (ADHD). One of the symptoms of this disorder is aggression. He would even randomly strike out in public at strangers.

We would eventually put Sean on medication, and this helped alleviate most of his aggression. The boys played better together, yet Cameron was not very happy being a part of our family. He was not used to structure, and he had a little brother who picked on him. Our family was now stressed to the limit. To make it through each day, I whispered prayers to the Lord before my feet hit the floor in the morning, and as I fell into bed each night, I would cry to God to get me through another day. Once again, in faith, I knew God would get us beyond this challenge. Through faith, I was developing patience as we continued to pray for wisdom every day.

A LONGING FULFILLED

Describe a time when you felt stressed.

_____

_____

_____

_____

_____

_____

_____

_____

_____

What was your response to that experience?

_____

_____

_____

_____

_____

_____

_____

_____

_____

Find a Scripture that overcomes stress and write it here.

_____

_____

_____

_____

_____

_____

_____

_____

_____

Each time you relive that memory or start to experience stress, start verbalizing your Scripture above.

10

A Long and Crooked Road

But the fruit of the Spirit is love, joy, peace, forbearance, kindness, goodness, faithfulness, gentleness and self-control. Against such thing there is no law.
—Galatians 5:22–23

Russ and Sean enjoying some bonding time

O ver the years, Sean would be diagnosed with peanut allergy, eczema, asthma, seizures, ADHD, Tourette Syndrome, obsessive compulsive disor-

85

der, oppositional defiance disorder, and a mood disorder. He was also a slow processor. In school, his reading challenges were later discovered to be dyslexia. It seemed every year, he was branded with a new diagnosis. I became very overwhelmed.

We wanted to find ways to help balance Sean's behavior with nutritional products and organic food. When he became totally unbalanced, we surrendered to medication. Having put Sean through chemotherapy was bad enough. I was very leery of putting Sean on medication to control his behavior, but we were desperate. I would now enter the world of dealing with the benefits and negative side effects of various medications.

Trips to the psychiatrist were part of our new monthly routine. This was no small event. Sean was often out of balance by the time we visited the psychiatrist. Often Russ would need to accompany me to keep Sean physically contained. To benefit from the best doctor, we drove all over Orange County. These visits were always stressful and draining.

One visit in particular still remains a vivid memory. Sean was about three years old. Russ and Sean were waiting in the playroom of the new psychiatrist's office while I filled out forms in the nearby waiting room. There was a big window separating the playroom from the waiting room. As I filled out the insurance forms, a lady waiting near me started chatting. She then looked over to the playroom window and started observing Sean. To no one in particular, she commented, "If only parents would learn to spank their children more!" Being in no mood for criticism, I replied, "If spanking worked, he would be a perfect child!" She was shocked to learn that was my child she was judging. Then in embarrassment, she whispered a little apology. I was on a new journey of judgment from observers. Thankfully, there would be many kind and compassionate people who would offer sweet encouragement. Those were the words that kept me afloat.

Sean was fortunate because he was steered into speech therapy at age two. The brain surgery had left Sean's right side of his body weak, and he would also need fine and gross motor therapy. He would require vision therapy as he was also peripherally blind to the right in both eyes. Sean's various therapy sessions were taking up a chunk of my time. I constantly felt overwhelmed by this intense schedule of school and therapy appointments.

Cameron had issues, too, but with time, both boys became more stable. We would switch to different doctors on a regular basis, and would continue driving all over the county to keep appointments. Eventually, we all got into a routine that created a rhythm we adjusted to.

Because special needs kids have many medical, emotional, and physical needs, we see doctors and therapists more often than the typical family. It would be many years before the boys' diagnoses were accurate. This is mainly because I constantly researched everything from brain injury to attachment disorder.

The blessing that resulted from all this chaos was my desire to help other parents. By the time each boy entered high school, we had to sue the school district for the boys' needs to be met. It was just after this time that I decided to become a special education advocate. I was overjoyed that I was able to pass on my knowledge and experience.

Although the stress of dealing with many more years of various therapies would be in the boys' future, God also gave me more gifts for my benefit, like the fruit of the spirit. These blessings were slowly transforming me from insecure and stressed out to peaceful.

A LONGING FULFILLED

Describe a time when you felt overwhelmed.

_____

_____

_____

_____

_____

_____

_____

_____

_____

What was your response to that experience?

_____

_____

_____

_____

_____

_____

_____

_____

_____

Find a Scripture that overcomes being overwhelmed and write it here.

_____

_____

_____

_____

_____

_____

_____

_____

Each time you relive that memory or start to experience feeling overwhelmed, start verbalizing your Scripture above.

11

King's Kids

And I will give eternal life to them, and they will never perish; and no one will snatch them out of My hand.
—John 10:28

Cameron and Sean enjoying some brotherly love!

It took me a few years to understand that I had a child with special needs. About the time I was coming to this realization, I knew I needed to take Cameron to a neurologist as well. He was showing some signs that I was already familiar with. At age six, Cameron was diagnosed with ADHD, and we needed to start him on medication as well.

He would also require some counseling to heal from his lack of care in his first couple of years. Because Cameron had gone a longer time without a stable family, he had to deal with many hurtful issues. With time and love, we began to see a happier child.

One morning, as he brushed his teeth and looked into the bathroom mirror, I heard him singing, "I love you, you love me, we're a happy family!" My heart completely melted with love and compassion for this very special child that God gave us. Even with all the challenges of Sean's aggression and his own issues to deal with, he felt loved!

It was during this same time period that I heard him listening to one of the Christian songs sung by kids that quote the Scripture from Revelation 3:20, "Behold, I stand at the door and knock. If anyone hears My voice, and opens the door, I will commune with that person and they will with Me." He asked me what this meant. I explained that Jesus is always ready to be invited into our hearts. Once we invited Him in, and professed that we believe He is the Son of God and that He died for our sins, we could live with Him forever in heaven. We are saved from eternal separation from God in the next life. While on earth, He showers us with the abundant life.

Cameron immediately told me he wanted to ask Jesus into his heart, so I excitedly prayed with him and he repeated the words out loud. I rejoiced with Cameron and with heaven on that day! Cameron would now forever be with us, in this life and the next. It wouldn't be long before Sean would say the same words. Our dear friend Robert baptized the boys at church with his wife Kay, Russ, and me looking on with tears of joy!

We met "Uncle Robert" and "Aunt Kay" at church. They were two very special people that God wove into our lives. Robert's best gift was helping us in the OICU years prior. Another precious gift they gave us was watching the boys to give us breaks. Kay prepared many meals for us over the years, which were always nutritious and delicious! Kay showered the boys with birthday and Christmas gifts. These were faith-building gifts that reflected the beautiful spirit of faith that shone in their hearts. Under Robert's guidance, the boys made Russ and me a darling white picket love-bench for our anniversary. They have constantly blessed us, and for their love and support, we are deeply grateful.

Going to church was always full of tension. Many Sundays, Russ and I would drop off the boys to their classes and would just be settling in for the sermon when our "Kid-Pager" would buzz, alerting us that we needed to check on Sean. He would be so disruptive that we would need to leave church. This was our routine for about a year before I realized I needed to pull Sean out completely. I started praying for a way to allow at least Russ, Cameron, and I to attend church.

My prayers were answered when one of my neighbors heard about our plight. Although she was a Christian, Sandy was not currently attending church, so for the next few months, we three were able to attend church together.

One day, Sylvia from church, called me. She wanted to brainstorm with me about how to accommodate Sean at church. We came up with an idea of starting a disabilities class, but I would need to pray about it. I was fearful of this idea. Where on earth would I find the time to run a successful ministry? I felt I was just surviving one day at a time. Life with my two boys was extremely challenging.

A week later, our church presented a program about an amazing woman who was a paraplegic. Her name was Renee Bondi. While she gave her beautiful testimony, she sang the words from Joshua 1:9, "Have I not commanded you? Be strong and courageous. Do not be afraid; do not be discouraged, for the LORD your God will be with you wherever you go." There was a quickening in my spirit. I knew instantly that God would take care of all the details if I would just trust Him and boldly take a leap of faith. I knew I was meant to start a brand-new ministry at my church. I shared my ideas with the church staff and presented my vision and my goals. I was very enthusiastic about initiating my ideas. I was also excited about the prospect of being able to worship undisturbed with my husband again. How great that we could offer this same opportunity to other couples with special-needs children. And the kids would get more enjoyment out of attending as well.

I coordinated the ministry called "King's Kids" successfully until we transferred to a new church home in 2009. It is still operating today and for that, I am very grateful!

Our current church has a well-established disabilities ministry and has blessed our family many times over the years! Connie and Alise have provided support for us moms, and they plan social activities for our adult sons and daughters with special needs. I am beyond grateful!

A LONGING FULFILLED

Describe a time when you weren't in control of your circumstances.

_____

_____

_____

_____

_____

_____

_____

_____

_____

_____

What was your response to that experience?

_____

_____

_____

_____

_____

_____

_____

_____

_____

_____

Find a Scripture that shows how to let God be in control.

_____

_____

_____

_____

_____

_____

_____

_____

_____

Each time you relive that memory or start to experience feeling you can't control your circumstance, verbalize your Scripture.

12

Of Disruptions and Delights

You then, my child, be strengthened by the grace that is in Christ Jesus.

—2 Timothy 2:1

A trip to the Monarch Preserve provides an
adventure and a teachable moment

R ounding the last corner of our destination, our
two boys started cheering as my parent's home on
the central coast of California came into view. The
four-hour drive from Southern California was only pleas-

ant once we started driving through Ventura Beach, where the view of the ocean calms the soul. Now unpacked and enjoying each other's company, we started to discuss our vacation plans. Grandpa Bud cheerfully announced, "We simply must go visit the Monarch Butterfly Preserve!" My stepdad, Bud, always had fun outings to suggest. Our boys loved visiting Grandpa Bud and Grandma Helen!

With the breakfast dishes now washed, we were gathering sweaters and putting on shoes. Sean wanted to wear his brand-new cowboy boots. Once slipped on, he proudly clopped outside, making as much noise as his little feet could make. We loaded into the van and zoomed off to our destination just minutes away. I was very excited to share this adventure of nature. Butterflies and transformation make an interesting lesson, and I was hoping to make this day a teachable moment for the boys.

Spying out the car window, Sean gleefully announced, "We're here! Let's go!" Once inside the preserve, the first thing I noticed was the sound of silence. I felt like we were in church. There was a feeling of reverence and awe in this outdoor sanctuary. Everywhere you turned, thousands of butterflies were clinging to the leaves of the eucalyptus trees. It was an amazing sight!

My mom offered to watch Sean for a few minutes so Russ, Cameron, and I could enjoy some peaceful moments. I was gazing at some monarchs, lost in the fascination of their beauty and delicacy. Suddenly, I heard a group of people gasp, "Oh no!" I immediately felt a sickening heaviness, a reaction from having experienced many times when Sean acted out impulsively. I spun around to see a group of people gathered in a tight circle. As I walked closer I heard someone exclaim, "I can't believe he did that!" Now I was certain it was Sean. Suddenly, my mom and Sean emerged from the circle of onlookers.

She explained to me how they had all been gazing at a monarch that had landed on the cement. Everyone was gathered around it to enjoy nature's show. Sean had suddenly popped into the center and ferociously smashed the butterfly with his efficient cowboy boots! That's when the crowed simultaneously gasped in horror!

After the crowd's negative comments, my mom defended Sean by saying, "This is what we teach our kids: to smash a bug with their shoe! In his little mind, that's all he was doing!" That's when she and Sean scurried out of the circle of judgment.

My first reaction was to say, "Let's get out of here!" But after reviewing what my mom had told the crowd, I realized this was a teachable moment on grace. I bent down and hugged Sean and kissed his soft cheek, reassuring him of my love. I explained some boundaries so that we wouldn't repeat that lesson again. I swallowed my pride, stood up, nodded to the circle of people still staring in disbelief, and we walked on to continue enjoying God's beautiful creation of the monarch butterfly.

I was able to offer a teachable moment after all by remaining calm during this disruption and offering grace. I was rewarded with the benefits of deep delight!

A LONGING FULFILLED

Describe a time when you experienced criticism.

_____

_____

_____

_____

_____

_____

_____

_____

_____

What was your response to that experience?

_____

_____

_____

_____

_____

_____

_____

_____

_____

Find a Scripture about grace (unearned love) and write it here.

_____

_____

_____

_____

_____

_____

_____

_____

Each time you relive that memory or start to experience someone judging you, start verbalizing your Scripture above.

13

Pauly Pockets

Your love has given me great joy and encouragement, because you, brother, have refreshed the hearts of the Lord's people.
—Philemon 1:7

Paul with Sean and Cameron

When our kids were young, we sometimes got together with our friends, Paul and Lisa. Our boys were near their girls' ages, and, to our surprise, they played well together. Social engagements were a rarity for us because of Sean's aggression.

Getting out socially with Russ was difficult as well. Babysitters didn't last long at our home. They would get overwhelmed by the boys' many challenges. But one friend gets my Perseverance award. Suzette lovingly offered to watch the boys for months so Russ and I could attend marriage counseling. She was one special friend with acts of kindness that we will always be grateful for!

Since our social outings were a rarity, it was always great fun getting together with Paul and Lisa. Sean took a great liking to Paul, and before long, he graced him with the name, "Pauly Pockets." I know this tickled Paul. None of us to this day know why Sean picked this nickname, but I know it was done with great affection. Each time we would leave to go home from a get-together, Sean would say, "I love you and I like you!" This melted Paul's heart. He talked about how we often say, "I love you" to someone, but we rarely say, "I like you!" Sean's little quirkiness tickled our funny bone regularly.

One day, Paul came over to drop off an item. I was in the middle of fixing my curtain, standing on one of our dining room chairs. We have a cushion on each chair. This day my balance seemed off. It felt like I was stepping on a mound. I pulled up the chair cushion and there was a very old hamburger bun stuck to the chair. Simultaneously, we vocalized our disgust. I explained that Sean has always loved putting objects between things. After a good laugh, I tried to erase that memory!

I have no idea why to this day, but Sean displayed very odd behavior on the day Lisa helped me by watching Sean in the waiting room while I ran in for my mammogram. Sean was sick and there was no way I was canceling the appointment I had made months ago. I knew I'd be in the back room for no more than fifteen minutes.

We entered the cramped waiting room and I got Sean occupied with a coloring book. Lisa must have kept thinking, "How hard can this be? It's only for fifteen minutes!" As I disappeared for my appointment, Sean thought it would be fun to make a run for it. He zipped out of the waiting room before Lisa even blinked an eye. She bolted after him and gasped as she saw him run into the open elevator. Before she caught up to him, the elevator door closed! She saw that it was going up, so she high-tailed it up the flight of stairs. As the door opened, she grasped his wrist, rode the elevator down, and they walked back into the waiting room.

They barely got settled when Sean got down on all fours and started crawling toward an elderly lady. Sean spied her sparkling sandals and started kissing her toes! The lady was so shocked that she quickly gathered her belongings and ran for the door, forfeiting her appointment with no thought.

After the poor lady left, Lisa asked Sean to sit by her, and he wouldn't comply. So she stood by him, holding his wrist. No more escaping this time! Then he started licking her arm, probably hoping she'd let go. But my faithful friend held on to him firmly until I reappeared in the waiting room! I was relieved to see them both waiting nicely for me. I had no idea of their adventures until we were back in the safety of my home. My thankfulness for Lisa's sacrifice was made even sweeter. I remember this incident with a mixture of horror and laughter! The uniqueness of my son has always been a constant source of surprises.

Over the years, Sean has tested us to our limits. But he has also brought a lot of hearts good cheer with his unique personality. Our memories are bursting with laughter!

A LONGING FULFILLED

Describe a time when you experienced a lack of joy.

_____

_____

_____

_____

_____

_____

_____

_____

What was your response?

_____

_____

_____

_____

_____

_____

_____

_____

Find a Scripture that describes how to obtain joy.

_____

_____

_____

_____

_____

_____

_____

_____

_____

Each time you relive that memory or start to experience feeling a lack of joy, start verbalizing your Scripture above.

14

Flying on the Floor

God is our refuge and strength, an ever-present help in trouble.

—Psalm 46:1

Sean and Cameron are posing with a
race car from Disney World

We were seated in the front row of first class when the stewardess announced that we were a Make-A-Wish family flying to Disney World. Everyone clapped and cheered for us and we felt special.

Although everyone knew we had a child with special needs, the next incident shocked us all, including me.

Sean had vestibular challenges. This meant that his mind and body did not properly interpret the force of gravity. He wouldn't walk up the steps to the slide, fearing the ride down, or get on the swings at school.

You can imagine the risk of putting a child with these challenges on a vehicle that defies gravity. The moment the plane lifted off the ground, Sean grabbed my arm and had a look of terror on his face. As the plane began to ascend, Sean ripped off his seat belt and dove for the floor. He began screaming. One might have thought his hair was on fire from hearing his terrifying cries. I was completely surprised and didn't know how to comfort him or convince him that he was all right.

The stewardess walked swiftly toward our row and asked how to help. I replied that Sean had gravity issues and was terrified. Thankfully the ascending plane leveled off quickly and we were able to get Sean back in his seat. The descent of the plane did not cause the same reaction, and we all breathed a sigh of relief.

Our vacation was a gift, compliments of the Make-A-Wish Foundation. To make the presentation more fun, they ordered a limo to pick us up from our home and then they drove us to Goofy's Kitchen a few miles away, near Disneyland. We had a delightful breakfast, complete with Disney characters wandering around to give signatures and a photo opportunity.

We were very thankful for the gift to Disney World, but we worried about not having any extra spending money. Of course the Make-A-Wish friends didn't forget and presented us with a big check just for that purpose.

From the Florida airport, we drove our rental car to Give Kids the World. This was a magical little "town" created just for the visiting Make-a-Wish families. We had a roomy duplex to live in for one week. In this village, there were little eating areas, an ice-cream sundae parlor, a game area, a swimming pool, and a fishing pier—just about everything a child could desire! All this was free to the families.

Each day brought new adventures. Sean and Cameron loved exploring daily for lizards right near the duplex. Every evening, when we returned from a day of adventure, there would be piles of gifts left on our dining room table. Although it was April, it was Christmas every day.

Ironically, we would be at Disney World for about two hours before Sean would tucker out. It was hot, steamy, and very crowded. He would beg us to take him back to our "home" so he could hunt for lizards and go swimming.

At Epcot Center, we never made it to the international area, much to my disappointment, but once again, lizard-hunting won out. The boys got along beautifully, and we felt like we were in heaven! We will always be grateful to the Make-A-Wish Foundation for allowing us to create beautiful memories.

Coming home on the jet, I dreaded the flight take-off. Although Sean cried and grabbed my arm, it was not a total freak-out experience this time. I was very thankful because we were in coach, and no one knew we were a family with special needs.

Just as I thought we had conquered the worst of our flying nightmare, we started descending to LAX in Los Angeles. Sean had been fast asleep, and this wake-up call startled his senses. He started screaming in staccato fashion. A man a few aisles up turned around and gave us an angry look. I've seen that look a million times. Translation: "Can't you control your child?" I feebly mouthed an "I'm sorry!" and then the plane was on the ground.

Thankfully, Sean would eventually have therapy to address his vestibular issues. It's called sensory integration therapy. We were amazed that it not only gave him the ability to enjoy slides and swings, it opened up new territory for him. He now rides on the fastest and scariest roller-coasters! Maybe I need that therapy.

About a year ago, I was returning from a flight and was waiting for my shuttle to drive me home. I was waiting with a group of ladies and we started chatting. It turned out that they were all Make-A-Wish volunteers going to an annual convention. One other mom and I couldn't believe we were surrounded by the angels that granted our kids such special wishes. Once inside the van, we both told our stories, and they thanked us profusely. They rarely get to hear the details about the trips they send the families on. We really made their day, and how happy I was to be able to give back in this small way.

A LONGING FULFILLED

Describe a time when you experienced weakness.

_____

_____

_____

_____

_____

_____

_____

_____

_____

What was your response to that experience?

_____

_____

_____

_____

_____

_____

_____

_____

_____

Find a Scripture that describes strength and write it here.

_____

_____

_____

_____

_____

_____

_____

_____

Each time you relive that memory or start to experience weakness, start verbalizing your Scripture above.

15

Firemen in Pajamas

Let the Light of the Lord shine upon me.
The LORD fills my heart with joy! I sleep in peace
because the LORD makes me dwell in safety.
—Psalm 4:6–8

I t never failed. The majority of medical emergencies occurred in the middle of the night. This was an area of extreme frustration for me as I was usually the parent that would accompany Sean to the ER. Russ worked a stressful full-time job with a long, daily commute. He needed his sleep more than I did. Being older parents to begin with made this task all the more challenging.

As a new parent, calling 911 was terrifying. I would be shaking and had a hard time controlling my emotions. The famous question from the operator, "What is your emergency?" would bring me to my knees in fear. I could see it happening before me, but to verbalize it made it a reality that was hard to bear.

Sean's various emergencies from having allergic peanut reactions to grand mal seizures made these calls necessary. Because Sean had perceptual challenges, his reaction to pain was exaggerated. Making the decision to call was difficult because I knew each trip to the ER would be a six-hour time commitment, so I knew I needed to be right.

When I dialed 911 for one of the first times, Sean was having difficulty breathing. He was about four. I was so scared! I blurted out the emergency between sobs. The fire department arrived quickly and administered oxygen. They quickly loaded Sean up into the emergency vehicle and sped off for the hospital. After six hours, he was stabilized and was able to return home.

I could not figure out what happened. After digging through the kitchen trash can later that evening, I retrieved a microwavable box lunch. As I looked at the front of the cardboard box . . . I shuddered! There was a picture with the words, *Peanut Butter Brownie*. I was so shocked! Sean was highly allergic to peanuts! I had fed him a meal that could have killed him. I was mortified. From that moment on, I learned to read every single ingredient on every single food item that enters our home. That was a mistake I would not repeat.

Our city's fire department knows us by name. I'm certain they also know my various sets of pajamas because our calls usually come around midnight. It's very humbling to be standing in a room full of uniformed giants (I'm five feet tall) in your pajamas.

When the firemen were standing in my son's room, checking his vitals and asking me for his medication and insurance information, I would be standing in awe of them. They are truly my heroes. Knowing Sean was being taken care of by someone much smarter than I am was very reassuring.

What did I learn from all these night-time events? I now own nothing but beautiful pajamas, made of cheery fabric, and one for each day of the week!

A Longing Fulfilled

Describe a time when you felt embarrassed.

_____

_____

_____

_____

_____

_____

_____

_____

_____

What was your response to that experience?

_____

_____

_____

_____

_____

_____

_____

_____

_____

BETSY KAY RIDGWAY, M.S.

Find a Scripture that helps you feel secure and write it here.

_____

_____

_____

_____

_____

_____

_____

_____

_____

Each time you relive that memory or start to experience feeling embarrassed, start verbalizing your Scripture above.

16

Stewart Little in Stitches

God is our refuge and strength,
a very present help in trouble.

—Psalm 46:1

Stewart Little with one remaining stitch above his eye

As a child, one of Sean's favorite sleeping buddies was the stuffed mouse, Stewart Little. He loved the movie. He had to have his mouse accompany

119

him just about everywhere we went. Cameron loved his Tigger, but wasn't as obsessed as Sean.

Having a favorite security item brought its risks. If it went missing, there was usually a meltdown around the corner. On one visit to see the grandparents four hours away, we had a taste of this risk. With our wonderful trip completed filled with fun memories, I had stacked all our vacation belongings on my mom's living room couch, ready to be packed in the car for our departure. As we finished this task, I did the usual once-over, looking one last time in each room. Satisfied we had all our necessities, we headed for home.

Halfway home, Cameron asked, "Where's my Tigger?"

I replied, "I had him sitting on the couch ready to be packed in the car before we left." I saw tears pooling in his eyes. "Can you look in the back to see if he's there?" I asked.

Cameron eyed the contents of the backseat and looked back at me, bewildered. "He's not there! Where is he?" I heard panic rising in his voice.

I reassured him, "Don't worry, we'll find him!"

After dialing my mom, I asked her to look around for our MIA Tigger. She said she would call me right back. Cameron was crying and we had at least two more hours of driving time. I sent a quick prayer heavenward!

My phone rang five minutes later, and my mom excitedly told me she had found Tigger! He had been stuffed between her couch and the wall. "Hmmm, I wonder how he got there?" Now I was looking at Sean, who had a guilty grin on his face. Yep, I knew he was the culprit. His favorite thing to do was stuff items between things. He had been doing this since he was two years old.

I reassured Cameron that Grandma would mail it to us. Cameron settled down and I praised him for this. I then wondered, *Why do kids have to become so attached to one thing?* As Pooh might say, "It's such a bother!"

When Stuart Little became Sean's favorite go-to toy, I decided to arm myself. I bought two more replacements! Little did I know that Sean had an uncanny ability to truly "know" his little mouse by heart. When his stuffed mouse went missing one day, I retrieved the spare with the exact set of pajamas and announced that I had found him. Sean cautiously accepted the mouse and started inspecting him. He then announced to me, "This is not my Stewart Little!" After tears and an in-depth search, mercifully, the original one was found and peace once again reigned.

One day, as Cameron and Sean were playing across the street in the neighbor's driveway, I suddenly heard the "I'm hurt" crying. I rushed over to see Sean's forehead dripping with blood. He had run into the neighbor's propeller blade on their boat, so off to Urgent Care we went!

Once there, the doctor announced that Sean would require stitches. Sean immediately asked if Stuart Little could also have stitches above his eye, just like his. The doctor chuckled and complied. To this day, Stuart still has his stitches. I should say one stitch. That's all that's left after years of loving and snuggling that little mouse face.

A Longing Fulfilled

Describe a time you felt insecure.

_____
_____
_____
_____
_____
_____
_____
_____
_____

What was your response to that experience?

_____
_____
_____
_____
_____
_____
_____
_____
_____

Find a Scripture that overcomes insecurity and write it here.

_____

_____

_____

_____

_____

_____

_____

_____

_____

Each time you relive that memory or start to experience insecurity, start verbalizing your Scripture above.

17

Police Dripping with Pancakes

*My son, keep your father's command and do
not forsake your mother's teaching.*
—Proverbs 6:20

Sean was about ten the first time I had to call for police assistance. Like the fire department, the police department became very familiar with our family! Both boys have had their share of familiarity.

That particular day, for whatever reason, Sean refused to take his morning medication. Sean was usually on two or three psychotropic medications to control his behavior. Skipping them was not an option!

This particular morning started like any other, but Sean would simply not take his meds. Without them, he could easily have a meltdown. After thirty minutes of trying all my tricks, in complete frustration, I dialed 911. I'm sure the operator thought I was a nut job. More "humility training" for me!

As the very large policemen entered my home, I knew Sean would comply. Their large presence even intimidated me a little. I led them to Sean's room. He was hiding under the covers. I asked, "Sean, why are you under your covers?"

He replied, "I don't want to go to jail." The police chuckled and started talking with Sean. I retreated to the living room. I was nervous, but figured this wasn't their first rodeo show.

Sean had been acting out with gusto. I told the police that with medication and food, he would settle down. As they successfully convinced Sean to take his meds, I entered the kitchen to finish preparing his breakfast. The police brought him out into the living room as I set down his pancake and bacon breakfast. He immediately started throwing a few pieces of pancakes at the officers. I was mortified! The police talked sternly to Sean and he began to eat.

They made small talk with Sean to pass the time so he would finish his breakfast. After I cleaned off his sticky fingers, the officers stated that they would leave now that Sean was compliant and calm. As they neared the front door, one of them quietly commented to me that he had never witnessed such a quick turnaround of behavior.

There would come a day when I would have to purchase a solid bedroom door with a deadbolt, regular locking handle, and extra sturdy hinges. When Sean would become aggressive in the future with his bigger body, this would be my only defense. The door would be replaced on a regular basis. Calling the police for help would become routine.

This is the nature of brain injury and children who lack verbal skills and impulse control. Their way of communicating their desires, if ignored, can sometimes be through aggression.

Now that Sean is older, he is learning how to control his anger. We are praying the day will come when he has full control, but until then, we try and stay in the "calm" zone.

A LONGING FULFILLED

Describe a time you felt extremely frustrated.

_____
_____
_____
_____
_____
_____
_____
_____
_____

What was your response to that experience?

_____
_____
_____
_____
_____
_____
_____
_____
_____

Find a Scripture that overcomes frustration and write it here.

_____

_____

_____

_____

_____

_____

_____

_____

_____

Each time you relive that memory or start to experience feeling frustrated, start verbalizing your Scripture above.

18

Schools and Other Scary Stuff

*Peace is what I leave with you; it is my own peace
that I give you. I do not give it as the world does.
Do not be worried and upset; do not be afraid.*

—John 14:27

Sean's first day of riding the school bus as a preschooler

ometimes I feel like we families of special-needs kids
live in a parallel universe. We engage in the same
activities, but in a way that would be totally foreign
to typical families unless they knew a family like ours.

The typical family sends their child to preschool for enrichment and social skills. They do so willingly; it is not required. On the other hand, we parents of special-needs kids have no choice. Our kids start into the public school system at age three. They are also expected to ride a school bus to school at this tender age.

Annually we are required to sit in a two-hour meeting with no less than four-to-eight professionals, and compose an individualized education program (IEP). The IEP lists the goals the child will work toward for the year.

The IEP "team" speaks a foreign language and passes out stacks of forms. Some documents contain test results that are meaningless to most parents. Signatures on many forms are required for agreement to everything discussed. I was one of the fortunate parents. To complete my master's degree, I took a class in statistics. This prepared me for the years of test results that would be presented every year.

I was grateful that the school system was trying to provide special education to meet the children's needs, but the typical parent enters this system with no knowledge of how it works.

This is one reason I became A Special Education Advocate. I wanted to advocate for the families who did not have the knowledge to ask for the necessary services for their special-needs kids. I was forced to sue the school district twice, one for each son. Although we prevailed in both lawsuits, I gained a lot of bitterness as well as knowledge about "how it all works."

After the five years I worked as a special education advocate, I was burned out. I prayed for God's direction for my next job. I felt led to create a website where I knew I could finally hand out a lifetime of learning regarding the school system, as well as inspire parents and caregivers. I wanted to bless parents with hope for their child's health and education. My Sparkling Hope website was inspired by the Scripture from Zechariah 9:16–17, "The Lord their God will save them on that day as the flock of His people. They will sparkle in His land like jewels in a crown. How attractive and beautiful they will be!" We *sparkle* with His *hope* when we trust in Jesus and live in His land of deep rest, refreshment and peace. (See Supplement A for website details.)

Another scary issue with the special education system is the transportation busses. I had a really difficult time releasing Sean into this program. I drove Sean for his first year of preschool. The teacher kept encouraging me not to be so protective of Sean. The second year, Sean rode the little yellow school bus, and new adventures were born.

Some adventures involved a season of throwing items out the school bus window. Some days, Sean needed to be strapped in to keep from hurting the other kids. But most days, Sean did well, and adjusted to this new routine. If the public school system would have put an aid on every school bus, a lot of the problems would have been solved immediately.

By grade four, Sean's behavior was becoming unmanageable, and we were told it was time to enroll Sean in a non-public school. He attended Buena Park Speech and Language Development Center for four years. This amazing school had a population based solely on special needs. This was a whole new world. Right on campus, they had a speech therapist, a physical therapist, a counselor, and specially-trained teachers. I became very involved with their parenting group and helped host fundraisers. I loved being a part of this world for four years. The staff was amazing!

By eighth-grade graduation, I had to make a decision about whether or not to send Sean back to public high school, or keep him in this more controlled environment. Observing the graduation ceremony made this decision a snap.

Sean was chosen to get up and read what he had written. His speech was amazing. There were about eight kids graduating. I could see that Sean no longer belonged in this school, and immediately enrolled him in the public high school's special education program. They had an excellent program and amazing teachers. Sean thrived in this environment.

After graduating high school, he enrolled in a fantastic transition program located on a college campus. He loved being around college kids. He also became friends with two aids who worked in his classroom. Kevin and Don are still in Sean's life, and we are deeply grateful for their friendship!

The next phase of Sean's life would be challenging. Day programs were created for adults with special needs. The main challenge for us was finding one with higher functioning adults with a stimulating program. Sean still needed to learn more in the area of adult living skills. We were not successful in finding a long-term program.

Amazingly, we discovered the adult education program tailored for adults with disabilities. This was a perfect match for Sean and it was on a college campus. This is where he is presently, and his confidence has grown tremendously.

We will always have hope for Sean's future. I don't worry as much as I did when Sean was younger and we were living through so many unknowns with the school system. Hindsight also has a way of making one more relaxed!

A LONGING FULFILLED

Describe a time when you felt worried.

_____

_____

_____

_____

_____

_____

_____

_____

_____

_____

What was your response to that experience?

_____

_____

_____

_____

_____

_____

_____

_____

_____

_____

Find a Scripture that overcomes worry and write it here.

_____

_____

_____

_____

_____

_____

_____

_____

Each time you relive that memory or start to experience feeling worried, start verbalizing your Scripture above.

19

Movers and Shakers

I have said these things to you, that in Me you may
have peace. In the world you will have tribulation.
But take heart; I have overcome the world.

—John 16:33

Our realtor Fred with Cameron, Betsy, Sean,
and Russ on moving day November 2002!

When Russ and I first purchased our town home, we designed a five-year plan to purchase a single-family dwelling. That five-year plan expanded into the fifteen-year plan. At the time, we didn't realize that we would be adopting our children. Nor did we have a clue about their many special needs. Both areas would be expensive, thus delaying our move into a home with a yard, and oh yes, a fireplace!

The day finally came when I heard God whisper, "It is time!" I knew in my heart that this meant it was time to move. We had tried unsuccessfully the year before to move. With God's guidance, we were able to sell and move into our new home within two months.

The process itself was a bit nightmarish. Sean was in the fourth grade and his behavior had caused the team of professionals at his school to recommend a non-public school. This new school transfer would take time as I needed to visit a few different schools. In the meantime, a home-school teacher would come for one hour per day. Of course, this was a joke. He wasn't getting his usual education for sure, but I knew this would be temporary. It's just unfortunate that this month-long excursion happened at the exact same time as our move from the town home.

Having to spend each day entertaining Sean and pack was pushing me dangerously close to insanity. We were able to enroll Sean in a fabulous school (the one mentioned in the last chapter), and we simultaneously managed to move all our belongings from one residence to the next. Toward the end of packing our things from the town home, I let the boys help me. They packed up all our shoes. But unfortunately the box never got labeled.

After our move, while surveying the mountains of boxes in our garage, I couldn't find the box of shoes. So in my slippers, feeling very sheepish, I drove to Target and bought a new pair of shoes. I explained to the checker why

I was wearing slippers. She laughed while I cringed. Later in life, I wouldn't let minor inconveniences like this bother me so much.

Within a few weeks, everything was put away and organized. Now I faced a new challenge. The boys' world just got bigger. How was I ever going to keep track of them with a whole block of houses? I felt there was only one solution, and it involved humility once again.

I decided to type up a letter that described our family, including the challenges our boys faced. After that, I marched up to each new neighbor with a smile, a plate of cookies, and my letter. Each neighbor was friendly as they thanked me for the cookies and for the courage to write the letter. This was the beginning of friendships that would form in our neighborhood.

A few weeks later, a few neighbors were gathered out front chatting when Stacie said, "I've always wanted to plan a block party. Would anyone be interested in helping me?"

I chimed right in, "Sure, I would love to help!" Thus began our block party tradition. A few years later, my neighbor, Linda, would help me organize the festivities. It's been fourteen years of planning and we just celebrated our twenty-eighth block party. Each year we celebrate the Fourth of July and a Christmas party. These parties have made us a very tight-knit group of neighbors.

One morning, a short time after we moved into our new neighborhood, Sean decided he wasn't quite ready to hop on board the school bus, and it would be arriving in about five minutes. Before I could even blink, Sean was out the front door and running up the street. I could no longer

BETSY KAY RIDGWAY, M.S.

catch up to him, so I decided to wait for him to return. When he didn't return, I began to sweat.

Then my cell phone rang. It was my neighbor halfway up the street. He could see Sean hiding in my neighbor, Fran's, bushes. I thanked my neighbor and headed up to Fran's. We already had a run-in with a broken light in her front yard. After the boys confessed to that little crime, I had them write an apology letter and deliver it to Fran.

Fran was extremely delighted to receive those notes. She never saw parents doing this anymore. She had been a special education teacher years ago, so at least my boys picked the right neighbor to mess with!

When I caught up to Sean, I asked him what he was doing in the bushes. He seemed very nervous. He told me he had spied a bee and tried to throw a rock at it, but he missed the bee and hit Fran's bedroom window! This would be a lesson for another day.

As soon as Sean departed on his bus heading for school, I called my handyman and made an appointment for him to come out and install a new pane of glass on Fran's house. She was very understanding and so friendly. This would be the beginning of a beautiful friendship.

Moving and transitions can cause a lot of distress. But I am thankful that we took the risk and moved into a new neighborhood. I consider each neighbor my good friend. I truly have a block of blessings!

A LONGING FULFILLED

Describe a time when you experienced distress.

_____

_____

_____

_____

_____

_____

_____

_____

_____

What was your response to that experience?

_____

_____

_____

_____

_____

_____

_____

_____

_____

Find a Scripture that overcomes feeling distressed and write it here.

_____
_____
_____
_____
_____
_____
_____
_____

Each time you relive that memory or start to experience distress, start verbalizing your Scripture above.

20

The Sky Is Falling

Humble yourselves, therefore, under God's mighty
hand, that He may lift you up in due time.
—1 Peter 5:6

As my friend opened her car door to step inside, a blue cloth floated down from the tree above and landed on her hood. Our eyes locked. Peering down at a pair of my husband's blue underwear, my mind blurred trying to comprehend nonsense.

Then in synchronous laughter, my friend and I threw back our heads and laughed with gusto. When you have special-needs kids like both of us, the "unexpected" is a regular visitor. What else can you do with a completely humiliating occurrence?

My son, the culprit, was standing nearby, joining in on the laughter. This helped make the heavy just a bit lighter. That which is humbling ushers in transparency. And the benefit? Deep friendships.

Like twins, we finished each other's sentences. She questioned, "Did I tell you that my daughter dropped her phone . . ."

I immediately responded with, "Down the disposal again?"

She replied, "Yes."

Then I began, "Did you know that Sean got suspended for throwing items out of the—"

She filled in, "—school bus window?" I nodded. And so it goes.

The most humbling fun occurs at the grocery store. When my son was younger, he often threw a tantrum because he was overstimulated by music playing and people walking everywhere. To the people standing near, he looked like a typical, out-of-control child. They were always quick to offer suggestions like, "Have you tried spanking him?"

With anger rising hot in my cheeks, I thought, "Seriously?" I had tried every method available to train this child! Pausing, I would remember that they were just ignorant about the world of special needs.

Eventually, I came up with a plan to help Sean calm down and simultaneously make others aware that he had special needs. I learned a few sign language gestures and taught them to Sean. They worked like a charm. At our next trip to the grocery store, people nearby realized I had a special-needs child, and they offered sympathy instead of criticism. Sean needed to use a different part of his brain to use the signing, thus causing him to be distracted, resulting in a calmer child. I tell other parents to use this sign language technique, even if they have to fake it. It will let others around know that you are dealing with a special-needs child.

No matter where we are, we will experience situations that humble us. I have found that responding with love and laughter is the best medicine for maintaining my peace and joy!

A LONGING FULFILLED

Describe a time when you experienced humiliation.

_____

_____

_____

_____

_____

_____

_____

_____

_____

What was your response to that experience?

_____

_____

_____

_____

_____

_____

_____

_____

_____

Find a Scripture that offers comfort for humility and write it here.

_____

_____

_____

_____

_____

_____

_____

_____

_____

Each time you relive that memory or start to experience humiliation, start verbalizing your Scripture above.

21

Medication Madness

Do not forsake wisdom, and she will protect
you; love her, and she will watch over you.
—Proverbs 4:6

My heart was racing as I pulled into the parking spot at my son's special-need's school. He was in the fourth grade and had been placed in this new school because of uncontrollable behavior right as we were moving into our new home. We were experiencing a season of sadness and confusion. We had tried a few different medications in an attempt to get Sean's behavior in balance.

The call from the school was frightening. Sean was out of control and I needed to come get him immediately. Thankfully, it was the end of the day. As I approached the front office, I heard howling that sounded like a wounded wolf. I remember thinking, "I'm glad that's not my child!"

As I neared Sean's classroom, the howling got louder. Now I was panicking in the realization that indeed it was my son, howling like a coyote. This was a sound I had never heard from him before, and I was terrified. I walked into his classroom to see Sean being restrained on the ground. He had been hitting, kicking, and spitting at anyone who came close. There had been no calming him down.

I reached into my purse for his emergency medication, for just this type of incidence. I realized I needed to wait a few more minutes before attempting to give him this medication. He would only spit it out now. After talking quietly to Sean for a few minutes, he started to settle down. I gave him his meds and continued to talk soothingly to him. Knowing he was in a heightened state of stress, I asked him no questions. Trying to reason with him at this point was futile, as it would be for anyone in the emergency mode.

Once at home, I did a quick search on his new medication, and I realized this one was not for him. The negative side effects did not outweigh the benefits. We made an emergency trip to the psychiatrist the next day to try a different medication. Within one week, we saw our old Sean again, sweet and lovable. I was hoping this was an experience I would never forget. Why? Because I had not properly researched this medication's side effects before agreeing to have Sean try it.

Now fast forward to the present. Sean was almost twenty-five and we were entering the fall season of 2017. His over-focusing behavior was driving us all a little crazy. So we asked the psychiatrist for a medication to help modify obsessive behavior. We were also working with a behavior specialist. Sean was living very successfully in an adult family home that he loved. This was the first home-away-from-home where he truly felt independent and loved. He was learning new skills, like riding the public bus, laundering his own clothes, and managing some daily money. Although his newfound freedom needed some tweaking, he was generally managing his life fairly well.

With the over-focusing issue, his team of supporters and I agreed it was time for medical intervention. But this was when I skipped a vital step! I forgot to do the research before adding it into his regimen. We were about to repeat a very painful lesson.

I rationalized some newly-seen anger and frustration to the craziness of the holiday season, but he didn't improve in January. In February, we decided to increase this new medication. Within a week, we started seeing a different Sean. He was showing regular aggression. He disobeyed rules and boundaries. He gave the silent treatment when told to do something. He engaged in risky behavior. His caretakers were starting to burn out and so were Russ and I. There seemed to be no answer in sight.

Then one evening, I was chatting with his main care-taker, Daniela. We were trying to figure out why he was once again acting out of control when I suddenly had a revelation. I immediately researched the contraindications of this newer medication. I was looking to see if it reacted negatively to the other medications he was on. Bingo! Right there in black-and-white, it warned of moodiness if mixed with his seizure medication. How could I have missed this research step? I had forgotten the lesson I experienced many years ago.

The doctors don't do it. The pharmacy does it once in a while. But you, as the parent or caregiver, must do it every single time. You must know your child's medications, their side effects, and how they interact with each other.

I was thinking about the definition of *madness* which is, "The state of being mentally ill, deranged, extremely foolish behavior, a state of frenzied or chaotic activity."

Check, check, and check! We had been witnessing all these definitions in Sean since being put on that medication! This medication literally made Sean "mentally ill" or the term we sometimes say, "crazy."

The chaos that resulted from this behavior spread from his adult family home, to school, to our home. He had driven us all a little crazy! Our special-needs kids often have very intense behavior, whether negative or positive, and medication can magnify this even further. It is vitally important that we take our role as parent very seriously when it comes to medication. We can't afford to sit back and trust the doctors without questioning them. Now with our smart phones, we can literally check on a med's contra-indications and side effects in a matter of minutes.

We had to make some dramatic adjustments, but in the end, Sean has benefited. He's recently learned how to ride the train independently, and he feels more grown-up. We're seeing our lovable son again. Now I pray this medication lesson has been learned for good. Writing about it should seal it in my memory!

A Longing Fulfilled

Describe a time when you lacked wisdom.

_____

_____

_____

_____

_____

_____

_____

_____

_____

What was your response to that experience?

_____

_____

_____

_____

_____

_____

_____

_____

_____

Find a Scripture that addresses wisdom and write it here.

_____

_____

_____

_____

_____

_____

_____

_____

_____

Each time that you relive that memory or start to experience confusion, start verbalizing your Scripture above.

Rattling and Rolling

The LORD makes firm the steps of the one who delights in Him; though He may stumble, he will not fall for the LORD upholds him with His hand.
—Psalm 37:23–24

Russ and I were in the kitchen one lazy afternoon in 2004. Sean was twelve years old and mature enough for us to let him go by himself to a neighbor's house to ask a question. He was due back at any moment. Suddenly, we heard a loud banging on our kitchen door that led to the garage. I thought Sean was playing around. What kind of game was this? As I swung the door open, I saw Sean at on odd angle with his head on the garage floor and his foot kicking the door. At first I couldn't comprehend what I was witnessing.

To my horror, I realized that Sean was having a grand mal seizure. I immediately went into "sergeant" mode and barked out orders to Russ, yelling, "Call 911, Sean's having a seizure!" I was petrified and had never experienced being in charge of someone with this medical emergency. I tore off my sweater and put it under his head so it would stop bouncing off the cement floor. The paramedics arrived within minutes and were taking Sean's vitals and asking me insurance and medical information. I handed them all the appropriate information while I was quivering inside with fear.

Sean was laid on the gurney and rolled into the waiting ambulance. With the sirens wailing, the medical team transported Sean to our nearby hospital. Russ and I followed, meeting them at the ER entrance. Sean was groggy and confused, but calm. He then fell asleep for a few hours. The MRI revealed no changes to his brain. For that, we were deeply thankful. The hospital released us with the recommendation to find a good neurologist. It would be years later before we found a neurologist that specializes in seizures, called an epileptologist.

Sean would now have to take seizure medications. They came with a list of side effects that were negative, but we had no choice. With each seizure, damage was done to the brain. For periods of time, Sean would lose some of

THE SONG OF MY HOPE

his memory, especially in the area of math. This was a very frustrating and frightening time.

It would be six months before Sean would finally have his seizures under control. This six-month period of time was extremely nerve wracking. I knew that if he had a seizure in his sleep, he could easily die. We knew of a family where this had happened.

My usual response kicked in with wanting to take control of this situation. I bought a baby monitor and set it up in his room. For the first few nights, I hardly slept. I had the monitor set up on my nightstand, complete with sound. Every time he turned over, I would stare at the monitor to make sure he was all right. By the fourth night, I decided to turn off the monitor and put it away. I simply had to give God the "night shift" if I was going to stay sane. This was difficult for me, but I prayed, "Lord, please watch over Sean at night and keep him safe. Please allow Russ and me to sleep like babies too!"

Because I grew up as a fearful worrier, I managed my life by trying to take control of every aspect. It would take me too long to realize that I was doing a poor job. After handing over my worries to God, I would feel much more peaceful. This season of seizures with Sean was no different. I knew I couldn't control the seizures outside of medication. But I could control how I reacted to this situation. I chose to give my worry over to God and let Him be in total control. This was trial by fire, and the reward was a peace that passes all understanding.

Sean remained stable until his senior year of high school, in the special education program. Then he started having grand mal seizures. Although they would only last for two months before we got him stable with the proper amount of medication, they were more frightening. In the past, the majority were petit mal. I called them "staring seizures." He would be frozen, stare, drool, and turn white as a ghost. These bigger seizures were terrifying and violent.

However, we were one of the fortunate families. Many children with seizures don't have a known cause. At least we knew that the area of Sean's damaged brain was the cause of the seizures. This knowledge was reassuring, yet the experience was still so alarming.

Despite the medical emergency, I knew God was next to us, holding us up. He gave me a great deal of comfort during this period of terror.

A LONGING FULFILLED

Describe a time when you felt terrified.

_____

_____

_____

_____

_____

_____

_____

_____

_____

What was your response to that experience?

_____

_____

_____

_____

_____

_____

_____

_____

_____

Find a Scripture that overcomes terror.

_____

_____

_____

_____

_____

_____

_____

_____

_____

Each time you relive that memory or start to experience that terror, start verbalizing your Scripture above.

23

Hairy Joy

But let all who take refuge in You be glad;
let them ever sing for joy.

—Psalm 5:11

Our sweet Max

Our counselor had just recommended that we buy a dog to help Cameron with healing from his childhood prior to being adopted. Cameron had trouble bonding and expressing his feelings of love. The counselor thought a dog would be the perfect "object of affection," helping him to eventually express statements of love to us.

Since Sean was allergic to dogs, we found a breed that had hair, not fur. People with allergies usually don't have a reaction with this type of dog. We made the plunge and bought a silky terrier.

It was a beautiful summer day in 2005, and Cameron and I were on our way to pick up our new puppy. Although I had two childhood dogs that I adored, I was apprehensive about owning a dog now. I knew the responsibility for his upkeep would eventually fall on my shoulders. I wasn't sure if I was strong enough for more burdens to be added to my long list.

However, my fears were put to rest on the drive home. Cameron decided to name our new puppy, "Max." Before we parked in the driveway, he was professing his love for Max. I was surprised that Cameron's heart was being transformed so quickly. I was thrilled!

This little puppy was about to change everyone's heart in the family. Dogs can sense your emotions. Max instantly knew that Sean was afraid of him. No matter how many times we tried to console Sean, his fear remained steady. He would attempt to pet Max, but once his hand drew near, his confidence left. He would let out a scream and start running. Of course Max loved this game! Sean would head for the safety of the couch, which was too high for Max. This routine was repeated countless times for about a month.

Finally, one day, I spied Sean petting Max as Cameron held him. I rejoiced. From that moment on, Sean was no longer afraid of Max. Once we successfully potty-trained Max, our lives fell into a comfortable routine with our newest family member.

Cameron continued to bond with Max. Everyone who met Max fell in love with him. I know God gave him a supernatural love, not only to minister to our family, but to all those who needed some extra love. He was just a bundle of love that brought us great joy!

With time, Cameron started showing more confidence. I know Max was part of the reason. It was his lack of good judgment that had Russ and me swimming in fear with the next adventure.

We had found a reliable caretaker for the boys through an agency. Our local regional center would pay for the services. We made a point of going out at least once a month. This gave us a break that was life giving.

At a nice restaurant with our friends Paul and Lisa one night, we sat chatting and enjoying the atmosphere. I decided to check on the boys by using a GPS locator on the phone. I quietly whispered to Russ that Cameron was not at home. After explaining our dilemma to our friends, we all watched the phone screen as we saw Cameron moving away from the home.

I called home to see what had happened. The caretaker said that Cameron's door was locked and he had loud music playing. I told him to go into the backyard and look into Cam's window. My suspicion was correct, as he was not in his bedroom. The caretaker also said that Max was missing. Now I was frightened.

We excused ourselves from our dinner date and reluctantly started driving home. We had waited a long time for this date, and I was angry that it ended at the beginning of the evening. But I was equally afraid for Cameron and Max. We had to go home to solve the mystery.

We put the pieces together after calling Cameron. He had decided that he wanted to show his girlfriend our new little dog. He had snuck out his bedroom window. Not using good judgment, he carried Max and brought no leash. How easily Max could have slipped out of his grip and then would have taken off running. God was protecting both of them! By this time, he had showed off Max and the girlfriend's mom was driving them home.

As I heard the car approach, I stepped out onto the porch. Cameron, Max, and his new girlfriend slowly approached. I was in no mood for polite exchanges and started questioning Cameron right on the spot. He then introduced me to his girlfriend. I apologized for my anger, and then she quickly departed with her mom. Our new "object of love" had been treated with recklessness, and I had to find a way to make this a teachable moment.

The funny thing is, I can't recall how I dealt with this problem, but my usual response to any training situation was using a natural consequence related to the offending behavior.

This next year would be the only time Cameron would have with Max as his behavior would spin out of control. We would have to take very radical action to save his life.

A LONGING FULFILLED

Describe a time when you felt a lack of joy.

_____
_____
_____
_____
_____
_____
_____
_____
_____

What was your response to that experience?

_____
_____
_____
_____
_____
_____
_____
_____
_____

Find a Scripture that describes joy and write it here.

_____

_____

_____

_____

_____

_____

_____

_____

Each time you relieve that memory or start to experience a lack of joy, start verbalizing your Scripture above.

24

A Whole New World

The LORD is near to the brokenhearted and saves
the crushed in spirit.

—Psalm 34:18

Several months after moving to our new home in the same city, I noticed Cameron was spending a lot of time behind his closed bedroom door. I knew this transition was very challenging for him, and worried that he might not be making a smooth transition with making new friends.

To add to this worry, he seemed to be doing quite poorly in his new school. One day, I asked him to describe his teacher and classroom. I was not prepared for his answer. He told me his teacher yelled at him and the other kids. She also berated him on a regular basis.

My Mama Bear hair stood at attention and I was ready to do battle! But first, I needed to calm down. Nothing would be accomplished if I called the principal and talked like a maniac.

I was a few minutes early for my appointment, and as I waited for the principal's door to open, my heart was pounding. Finally, she called me into her office. I laid out the argument that perhaps this teacher was burned out and needed a vacation after sharing what Cameron had told me. I wanted to appear reasonable.

The principal pretty much shut me down. I realized she had an obligation to defend her staff, but I was determined to solve this problem one way or another. I insisted that Cameron be transferred to another classroom. She complied.

His academic life calmed down, but another battle was bubbling to the surface right under our noses. With frequent trips to the principal's office regarding Cameron and marijuana, we realized that this was becoming a chronic problem. Eventually, we felt we had to put Cameron through a drug test at home. This was the worst feeling in the world, but we didn't want Cameron traveling down the same road as his biological mother. As grateful as we were to her for allowing us to raise her son as our son, we were always aware that DNA plays a strong role in addiction.

Cameron was in junior high when the drug problem really started to rear its ugly head. He attended two different junior high schools and barely made it through to the ninth grade. There were new friends coming into his life, and we were losing control of his free time.

Ninth grade was the end for Cameron's public high school attendance. There were too many behavior problems, so he started attending alternative schools. Before long, this became too difficult for Cameron to manage. His behavior at home was becoming more rebellious. Now he was starting to disappear for a day or two.

We would be frantic, and would file a missing person's report with the police. We did this routinely until he disappeared for two weeks. I cried myself to sleep at night. This was an intensely sad and confusing time for both Russ and me.

In desperation, I called Debbie, Sean's biological aunt, who also loved Cameron. I told her how long Cameron had been missing and how desperate we were to find him. I asked her to call me if he showed up to her home. Russ and I had come up with a plan to save Cam when we found him next. It would change all of us in the end. But it was a completely necessary plan. We did not reveal our plan to Debbie. We wanted to make sure it would be successful.

Debbie called us one afternoon a few days later. Cameron had turned up at her home. He was currently eating. I asked her if she could ask him to shower to stall for time so we could drive over there. She agreed. We immediately called our friend from church who we had previously agreed to come with us. He wasn't too keen on this plan, but he agreed anyway.

Russ, our friend, Sean and I sped over to Debbie's house, about fifteen minutes away. Our friend and Russ went into Debbie's home to retrieve Cameron. When he got into the car, I hugged him and said I was glad he was safe. He was unemotional, like a zombie. I was heartbroken, for I knew what was in store next.

As we drove in a different direction from home, Cameron asked, "Where are we going?" Russ replied that we were running an errand before going home. As we got closer to the hospital, Cam became agitated. He said, "I want to go home now!" We said we'd be going home shortly. As we departed the car, Cam asked, "Why are we at the hospital?" I think he knew deep in his heart what was transpiring.

Russ replied, "We are here to get you checked out by a doctor." In reality, this was the first step in our plan to save Cameron, but he felt we were betraying and rejecting him.

We had all waited till about 10:00 p.m. in the ER, with Cameron being aggressive. This was understandable because he was high on drugs, and he was being held captive. My mother's heart was breaking right in two. This tough love was just as hard on me as it was on everyone else. Cameron wasn't the only one suffering.

A private room was finally ready for Cam, so I sent everyone home and told them I would stay until the psychiatrist evaluated Cameron. They had to post the security guard right outside the door for my protection. It was going to be a long night. Cam was sitting on a patient table/ bed, and I was seated near the door. When I looked over at

Cameron, he looked so angry. I just kept praying for God to soften his heart.

Thankfully, I had grabbed some writing paper before we left to get Cameron. I started pouring out my pain on the paper, and my hand couldn't write fast enough. I just kept thinking back to the day we said we would adopt Cameron at the adoption agency. We weren't prepared for another child, yet we knew deep in our hearts that the boys, being half brothers, should be raised together. Our marriage suffered as a result, and eventually, we sought marriage counseling. We loved Cameron with our whole hearts, and we now had to display tough love like never before.

He couldn't see that our current plan was created out of love. We knew Cameron would have died had we not saved him. As I asked Cam a question, his hateful answer prompted the guard to come into our cubicle to warn him to speak respectfully to me. Cam settled back on to the plastic bed and seethed. I continued my flurry of words on paper to stay calm.

Around midnight, the psychiatrist came into the room to question Cam and me. It was in the wee hours of Friday morning when Cameron was finally admitted to the psychiatric unit of the hospital. I left with tears and a very heavy heart.

The next morning, it was time to implement the rest of our plan. I first needed to secure an educational loan. After that was completed, I needed to secure a residential treatment center for Cameron. I would need to find one that was out of state because Cam was a runner. In the State of California, they don't have locked doors, so there was no other choice. I called a few schools and they said Cameron was too hardened for them. I finally called Sagewalk, the wilderness school that was created to treat kids with drug and alcohol addiction. He was accepted.

A few hours later, my sister Pam called me from Nipomo, California, where my mom and my stepdad, Bud lived. Bud had been diagnosed with cancer and was in the last stage. My sister, Pam, bless her, had gone up there to help nurse him. My mom was too tired for this job. She called to tell me that Bud had passed on. While I was glad he wasn't suffering anymore, I was in survival mode and decided that I would have to tuck away my pain and cry later.

Right now, I needed to find professional transporters. They would take Cameron from the hospital to the airport and fly with him on the plane. Once he got to Sagewalk, their staff would take him the rest of the way.

As relieved as I was that the plan was now set in place, I was worried about the mounting cost. I reasoned that surely the school would reimburse us. We had discussed residential treatment centers (RTC) months prior. The school's response was always the same, "We have to wait until he hits rock bottom, with an arrest record." We were so angry that this was their approach. It was totally reactive instead of proactive. The school psychologist interviewed Cameron in the hospital. He completely agreed that he needed to be in a residential treatment center. But the school would not agree to pay for Sagewalk, which was $15,000 a month. We had to swallow the cost for two months. With the cost of the transporters and the first month's payment of the residential treatment center, the bill would be double that before we were through. We knew that this could bankrupt us, but we also knew we couldn't let Cameron die. We were literally in a fight for his life.

Cameron was so angry with us that he wouldn't let us visit him at the hospital. Debbie and Brian (Sean's birth aunt and birth dad) were the only people who Cameron would see. I knew he still had a deep bond with them, so I felt glad that he could receive comfort from their visit.

We had to make Cameron's future our priority. Our love and protection for Cameron ran deep. He was our son. No matter what, we were willing to have him hate us and possibly lose our home over this plan.

Even though it's been eleven years, I still write this story with tears. The sadness from this season will always be in a little corner of my heart. Cameron would spend two months at Sagewalk, then go on to spend the next few years in residential treatment.

At this point, I only wish Russ and I had joined Al-Anon sooner, but we were not steered in this direction. I would finally attend meetings years later and would learn a great deal. I learned that I am not responsible for another person's addiction, and I am not responsible for their happiness. For me, this was huge. I really took on a lot of guilt for the turn in Cameron's life back in junior high when he started on marijuana.

I still struggle with some guilt in the parenting department, but I've come to the realization that we did the best we could. I know with time, Cameron will come back to love us wholeheartedly. I pray for this every day. I want to feel connected to him again.

He currently has four beautiful children with Elizabeth Kate. (I'm Elizabeth Kay!) Her mom and dad help out tremendously. My support is limited because they live quite a distance away. I know that one day soon Cameron will be whole, fresh, and a brand-new person ready to live life to the fullest. This is my daily prayer, and he will have an amazing story to tell too!

A Longing Fulfilled

Describe a time when you experienced a broken heart.

_____

_____

_____

_____

_____

_____

_____

_____

_____

What was your response to that experience?

_____

_____

_____

_____

_____

_____

_____

_____

_____

Find a Scripture where God heals a broken heart.

_____

_____

_____

_____

_____

_____

_____

_____

_____

Each time you relive that memory or experience a broken heart, verbalize your Scripture above.

25

Legal Beagle

*For there is one God, and one mediator also
between God and men, the man Christ Jesus.*
—1 Timothy 2:5

From my bedroom, I watched the boys playing basketball next to the swimming pool. Because we lived in a small town home community, I had warned Cameron in the past about never kicking the basketball in the air, but his natural bent toward soccer made this rule unbearable.

I suddenly heard the sound of normal dribbling turn into a solid thud. My heart dropped! I knew Cam had just kicked the basketball into the air! The next sound was a bloodcurdling scream. I immediately raced down the stairs and across the alleyway to the play area. My mouth dropped open as I saw impending disaster.

A woman had been sunbathing just a few feet away from the fence that separated the basketball area from the pool. She was now sitting up and holding her head. The ball had landed on her head! She immediately sprang up, grabbed her beach towel, and muttered something unintelligible. I asked her which town home she lived in so we could make sure she was all right. She left, verbalizing something angry I couldn't quite understand, but I knew this was serious.

Later that evening, Russ walked over to her unit to check on her health. She informed him that she was going to sue us. Russ left shocked and dejected.

Upon hearing the neighbor's threat, Russ and I quietly discussed some of our options, none of which looked good. We were living paycheck to paycheck with little in savings. Instead of looking up a lawyer, we decided to go to our heavenly mediator, Jesus. We prayed a desperate, heartfelt prayer for a peaceful resolution to this matter.

This was the ultimate teachable lesson for Cameron and the basketball problem. He vowed never to do that again. For now, the basketball would remain in the closet for a week.

The next evening, Russ walked over to visit the woman again. Her husband was there and greeted Russ coldly. Russ knew a few words of their native language and spoke a greeting to them. This was the fire that warmed the ice!

Russ apologized again for Cameron's actions and offered to pay for their doctor bill. They agreed! Unbelievably, that was the end of the matter. Our prayer had been answered!

This experience ushered in the idea of how we could provide legal protection for our boys in the future. Through researching the topic, I came across "conservatorship" and realized this would be our answer. Cameron was too high functioning for this, but Sean was the perfect candidate.

However, it wouldn't go into effect until the child became a legal adult at age eighteen. When that time came, we hired a lawyer that specialized in this matter, and scheduled the court date. We sat in the court room all day, the lawyer, Sean, Russ, and I. We were the last ones called to come before the judge. Thankfully, it was a short process, and we walked out as Sean's legal conservators.

We would have the right to attend his doctor appointments, be in charge of all his records (educational, medical, legal), sign contracts on his behalf, decide where he resides, and speak on his behalf when necessary.

In our particular county, we do not have the right to insist on birth control, whether temporary or permanent. We also do not have the right to forbid him to marry. We hope he is able to be independent enough to marry someday. We don't see children in his future due to his level of functioning. Unfortunately, the law does not let us protect him. We pray he will come to this conclusion and take medical action.

Although it takes a lot of energy, time, and money to establish being a conservator, it is well worth it. It is the best way to protect your special needs adult. It has given Russ and me a sense of peace knowing we can still protect and guide him during his adult years. As for the situations out of our control, we still go to our heavenly mediator!

A Longing Fulfilled

Describe a time you encountered a legal problem.

_____

_____

_____

_____

_____

_____

_____

_____

_____

What was your response to that experience?

_____

_____

_____

_____

_____

_____

_____

_____

_____

Find a Scripture that addresses legal issues.

_____

_____

_____

_____

_____

_____

_____

_____

Each time that you relive that memory or start to experience anxiety over a legal matter, start verbalizing your Scripture above.

26

Scrambled Eggs in the Garage

The mouth speaks from the overflow of the heart.
—Matthew 12:34

I was taught the Lord's Prayer as a child (Matthew 6:9–13). For many years, I recited it by heart at bedtime with my parents; however, the prayer did not come alive for me until later in life. As a parent of special-needs boys, I have lived through many adventurous but painful experiences. During those times, I used the Lord's Prayer as my blueprint for becoming a better parent. I especially love the section on forgiveness. I have learned that as God forgives me of my everyday shortcomings, I need to live in a ready state of forgiveness.

One of Sean's challenges is problem-solving. His "solutions" often end up causing distress for my husband and me. One morning, as I was getting dressed, he spied one lonely egg in the carton. One of the symptoms of obsessive-compulsive disorder (OCD) is that you have an intense desire for everything to be even, neat, and tidy. Just one little egg in a carton was bothersome to Sean. In his mind, he was solving a problem by figuring out how to get rid of that one egg. He plucked the egg out of the carton, opened the door to the garage, and threw it as far as he could. After throwing away the carton in the trash he must have thought, *Problem solved!*

When I was finally ready to prepare Sean's breakfast, I searched for the egg carton. "That's funny," I remarked, "I know I had one egg left. I was going to use it to make your breakfast, Sean."

He looked up at me very innocently. "Have you seen it, Sean?" I asked.

He quickly confessed, "Sorry, Mom, I accidentally broke it." I asked him where the cracked egg was and he proceeded to give me a few different versions of the story.

I kept questioning him until the truth finally emerged. He then explained, "After I took it out of the carton, I threw it up into the rafters of the garage," as he demonstrated the lob. As a younger parent, my immediate reaction would have been predictable: anger. But over the years, I have learned to invest time each morning with the Lord. I've been transformed into a more loving and patient parent.

After peacefully responding, "Well, let's go look for it," we discussed different ways he could have responded to this problem that would have been more appropriate. I wanted this to be a teachable moment, not a time of shaming.

As many parents of young children know, this incident is not an unusual experience. But Sean was twenty-one, and I was still helping him solve these everyday problems. Thankfully, I was able to stay calm after we found the egg mess splattered on the unfinished wall by the lawn mower. I was relieved to see the egg had landed nice and low and all in one spot. It could have been so much worse!

I infused humor into recounting the experience later in the day. This allowed Sean to experience my forgiveness. How could I do any less when God has forgiven me for my sins? Mine are messier than broken eggs. Forgiveness is the tool that unlocked the door of my anger and allowed me to step through to overflowing peace and joy. Later that day, with forgiveness in my heart, words of reconciliation and restoration flowed from my lips as a bond of love enveloped us.

Who would have thought that a broken egg could usher in healing through forgiveness? By hiding the Lord's Prayer deep in my heart as a child, the seed of forgiveness grew so that I might follow the example that Christ laid out for me. I am thankful that Jesus taught me that God's ways are higher than my ways, and His thoughts are higher than my thoughts. As long as I lean on the Lord in the midst of my pain, I am able to live a more excellent life, full of hope and peace.

A Longing Fulfilled

Describe a time when you needed to forgive someone.

_____

_____

_____

_____

_____

_____

_____

_____

What was your response to that experience?

_____

_____

_____

_____

_____

_____

_____

_____

Find a Scripture that addresses forgiveness and write it here.

_____

_____

_____

_____

_____

_____

_____

_____

_____

Each time that you relive that memory or start to experience unforgiveness, start verbalizing your Scripture above.

27

The Summer of My Reconstruction

Be completely humble and gentle; be patient,
bearing with one another in love.

—Ephesians 4:2

Betsy is standing in front of her
nearly-completed kitchen

Toward the end of June 2015, Russ and I made a decision to remodel our kitchen as well as Sean's bathroom. The construction company estimated six weeks for our home to be completed. The long list of challenges woven into our project is where this story begins.

On the first day of the ear-splitting, dusty demolition, Russ called me from work to announce that he had slipped and was at the doctor's office getting examined. His recent knee injury was still healing and now his ankle injury landed him on crutches and pain pills. Adding to the stress, Sean was diagnosed with an ear infection that lasted three weeks, forcing him to be home with the construction chaos.

With the injured and ill-tempered men underfoot, I was already beginning to feel weary. It didn't help that each new appliance and fixture that arrived at our home was dented or scraped and had to be replaced. Having to reorder many items, I was already starting to feel overwhelmed.

During the chaos, I was leading a group of women at my church in a Bible study on joy. This helped me maintain my sense of sanity. I find my deepest joy springs forth from times of extreme difficulty and pain. This new Bible study was perfectly timed.

After living with no kitchen for six weeks, a house in chaos, and a week's stay in a hotel while our ceilings were scraped and walls painted, I was more than ready for some normalcy! We were poised and ready for the very last day of finishing touches. I knew I could handle one more day.

Russ and I were taking a short rest on Sunday when Sean called out for me in a panic, "Come quick! The toilet is overflowing!" I flew out of bed to see water running out of the bathroom and down the hallway. Barefooted, I slogged into his bathroom to turn off the water line. I then yelled to Russ to grab every towel in the house. After thirteen soggy towels were scattered like beach blankets on a crowded, sandy ocean front, I realized this was no ordinary overflow of the toilet.

Wondering how many millions of bacteria my feet were soaking in, I sloshed my way along to retrieve all the wet towels so I could begin decontaminating the floor. After an hour of clean up and feeling like a nervous breakdown was near, I flopped down on my bed and realized I couldn't go on without running to a source of comfort.

I'm ashamed to admit this, but my first thought was, "Where's Sean's Ativan?" I've never relied on medication for anxiety, but I was ready to begin! My anxiety and fatigue had co-mingled to form a tsunami wave of complete helplessness.

Thankfully, my next step was to run to God, the only way to find true comfort. I prayed a deeply desperate prayer. I was completely spent, broken, humbled, and ready to ask for help. About ten minutes later, I got out of bed, feeling enough refreshment to think about the next step.

I called my insurance company, and they completely rescued us. They not only remodeled Sean's bathroom again, they also refinished our hardwood floors throughout our entire home. They were forced to do this since there was no beginning or ending point, just one continuous floor throughout the home, except for the kitchen and bathrooms.

Before the floors could be refinished, we had a new problem. We had already moved out once. Now we would need to move out as though we were really moving! They placed a "pod" on our driveway, and moved absolutely everything out of our home. We would once again spend a few weeks at a hotel, which for us was no vacation!

I used to believe that God only gives us what we can handle. Now I know for a fact that is not true. Otherwise we would not "need" God. This whole construction project was way more than I could handle. Thankfully, I realized this in time to let God handle it!

What a difference this revelation has made in my life. I'm living more peacefully and have a lot more patience, even though the trials of life have not subsided. Right after we moved back in, Sean got hit by a speeding bicycle and needed a trip to the ER. Then a few days later, a huge fire broke out in our town causing Sean's asthma to flare up. This meant two more separate trips to the ER.

The Lord is taking real good care of us, day by day. I have concluded that more than the kitchen and bathroom got remodeled that summer. So did my faith!

A LONGING FULFILLED

Describe a time when you needed comfort.

_____

_____

_____

_____

_____

_____

_____

_____

_____

What was your response to that experience?

_____

_____

_____

_____

_____

_____

_____

_____

_____

Find a Scripture that leads you to comfort.

_____

_____

_____

_____

_____

_____

_____

_____

_____

Each time you relive the memory or start to feel overwhelmed, start verbalizing your Scripture above.

Hopscotch

I will teach you the way you should go; I
will instruct you and advise you.

—Psalm 32:8

Our special needs kids spend their educational lives and their residential placements hopscotching all over town. At age three, they will attend pre-school at the same school for two years. After that they might transfer to a new school for kindergarten. By the time Sean was in first grade, he was attending his third school. These kids get placed according to their level of functionality.

It's difficult enough for typical kids to make friends. Our kids usually lack social skills, making it more difficult to form bonds and make friends. When you add in the hopscotch factor, friendships are a rarity.

After a special-needs student graduates from high school, they then are enrolled in a program called Transition. This is a three-year program with life skills training at another school campus. It's also a time when the parents start planning for this young adult's future that is beyond the protection of the school setting.

When Sean was a senior in his special education high school, he began having grand mal seizures. These were frightening! Even more terrifying was the thought that it would happen at school where he might be out at a community site. The school arranged to have the students do volunteer jobs at various stores like the 99 Center Store, the local fabric store, and occasional short jobs at the pizza parlor. This would give them job skills with on-the-job-training.

They walked to these sites using the sidewalk adjacent to a heavily-traveled road with cars traveling at high speeds. I told the school about my concern of him walking next to the street with the possibility of having a grand mal seizure. Once again, the school would accuse me of being overprotective and would assure me they would be watching Sean closely.

Thankfully, this dangerous scenario never occurred. But once Sean was enrolled in the transition program located on a college campus, I was nervous when I learned they left the campus on a more regular basis, again walking next to a heavily-trafficked street. I prayed daily for his protection.

Once these kids turn eighteen, with eligibility, the local regional center will find housing for them. Some parents choose to keep their young adult at home. Sometimes, they never leave home until the parent dies. In our case, with Sean being aggressive, we chose to place him at age eighteen.

Sean's first experience in a group home was heartbreaking. He had been molested and was brave enough to tell the school nurse. This group home had proven that the staff was not capable of keeping Sean safe. He would come home to live once again until we changed the course of his living conditions. We kept praying for God's direction for the next season of Sean's living quarters.

Overall, his second group home seemed a better fit. There were only four clients, instead of the usual six, and they were all young people this time. Unfortunately, this home would prove unsafe as well, endangering his life on a number of occasions. We moved him back home again until we discovered adult family homes.

An adult family home is a more natural setting. A family chooses to bring in one or two clients into their home, to blend into their family activities. Although the first home did not work out, the second one was amazing. Daniela and her sister Ximena were natural caretakers. Eventually, Lina would move in when Ximena moved out. He lived there for eighteen months until his behavior deteriorated to the point where he would need a new home. It was most unfortunate that Sean was experiencing a negative reaction to a medication that caused him to be angry and moody. We were all going crazy right along with him!

He is currently in another adult family home, and we pray this home gives him stability and even more independent-living skills. Our hope is that Sean will be able to live in an apartment one day with support.

After a young adult has completed the transition program, there are three choices: a day program, a job, or more education. We knew Sean wasn't ready for a job, so we searched out day programs. He attended a handful, but with each one either the population of people was too low functioning or it wasn't stimulating enough for him.

What I discovered a few years after the completion of his transition program would be a gold mine! There was an adult education system with a special program for adults with disabilities. This was his new niche! We enrolled him, and he loved being on a college campus again. He has had a lot of former classmates in his classes. He was coming full circle.

When he completes this program in 2020, it will be time for his next season. We are hoping it will include a paying job. He has learned how to ride the city bus and the train independently, so he will always be able to get to his job.

His hopscotching with living arrangements and jobs will always be a part of his life. Change is difficult even for the most "typical" of us, but flexibility is an uncommon trait in the special needs population. It's particularly heartbreaking when our special needs adults have to leave a home because of their behavior. They bond with the family members, and they begin to think of the caretakers as their family. I pray for Sean's stability and peace every day!

A LONGING FULFILLED

Describe a time you needed guidance.

_____

_____

_____

_____

_____

_____

_____

_____

_____

What was your response to that experience?

_____

_____

_____

_____

_____

_____

_____

_____

_____

Find a Scripture where guidance is offered and write it here.

_____

_____

_____

_____

_____

_____

_____

_____

_____

Each time you relive that memory or start to experience feeling confused about your path, start verbalizing your Scripture above.

29

Siblings Unforeseen

Your Word is a lamp to guide me and a light for my path.
—Psalm 119:105

Russ and Betsy with their newest
family member, Brent.

When I think of our family, with our two special boys who God gave us the privilege of raising, I think of a family with many struggles, but stable with faith in God. We are definitely not your typical family!

When Sean turned eighteen, we knew we would have to find him a home where he had more supervision than we could give him. We were burning out from the years of dealing with Sean's aggression. Unfortunately, at that time, there were currently no homes available.

With the support of our local regional center, they provided us with workers who would help keep me safe when Sean would become aggressive. I am five feet and Sean was closing in on six feet, so I was relieved when they sent us a strong, young man named Brent, who had previous experience working with aggressive special-needs kids.

Brent arrived at 3:00 p.m. and departed at 9:00 p.m. He also worked Saturdays from 8:00 a.m. to 4:00 p.m. We personally hired him to attend church with us on Sundays to be Sean's companion. After Brent's contract ended, he volunteered to come to church with us to watch over Sean, and we were grateful!

At first I was uncomfortable having a stranger in our home, but eventually, Brent felt like family. We started inviting him over for the holidays, not to work, but just to hang around the family and enjoy each other's company.

One particular Christmas changed the course of our family forever. Brent had wrapped a present for us. When it came time to open it, he seemed a little nervous. After we opened the gift, we saw a framed picture of Brent from his high school graduation. He told us that there were only two of those pictures. His grandma had one and now we had the other. I was deeply touched! He said there was an accompanying letter, but he did not want us to read it until he left. The mystery was killing me!

Right after he left, I tore open the envelope. It was such a beautiful and heartfelt letter. He explained that he didn't have a loving family growing up. He had felt so comfortable around our family for the last year that he wanted to join us. He wanted to call us Mom and Dad. I was astounded. I guess when you are in the midst of constant stress, it's harder to see the good times, but Brent saw them, and he wanted to meld into our family.

We chatted the next day. We told him we would love to have him be our son. He didn't want to change his name or be legally adopted. He just wanted to soak in the love and joy that our family had to offer. Our hearts were once more expanded to include another family member. That was 2009. He has been considered our son ever since.

Another delightful experience occurred a few years ago. Cameron had located three of his four younger biological sisters. They were Cameron and Sean's half sisters through their birth mom, so we set up a date to meet them.

They came for a family style dinner at our home and Sean was in heaven! They had previously met Cameron, and he had already moved out of state. Sean was ecstatic that he had them all to himself!

They are lovely and beautiful. I'm so glad we got to connect with them. Cameron and Sean communicate with them regularly through texting and Facebook. During this first meeting, I realized for the first time that they did not have their mom around for long. She had died quite young from cancer. It was all so sad!

For Mother's Day that year, I combed through my files and made a copy of all the letters to and from the birth mom, as well as all pictures of her that she had sent. I sent each girl her own package of letters and pictures. My heart just burst with love as I mailed them off. I felt like I finally got to thank the birth mom in a deeper way. The two gifts that she gave Russ and me were treasures like no other. We would never be able to repay either of the biological families for the love they lavished upon us through the adoption of Cameron and Sean. The best thing we could do is love the boys with all our might! I know she is smiling from heaven.

A LONGING FULFILLED

Describe a time when you needed help making a big decision.

_____

_____

_____

_____

_____

_____

_____

_____

_____

What was your response to that experience?

_____

_____

_____

_____

_____

_____

_____

_____

_____

Find a Scripture that offers help when making an important decision.

_____
_____
_____
_____
_____
_____
_____
_____

Each time you relive that memory or start to experience confusion about a decision, start verbalizing your Scripture above.

30

Fly Away, Birdie

For He will command His angels concerning
you, to guard you in all your ways.

—Psalm 91:11

I watched Sean walk toward his classroom with
a lump in my throat, but a smile in my heart!

W e know not all baby birds fly independently the
first time. If they fail, it usually means being
maimed or instant death. It seems so cruel, but

then again, I freely acknowledge I'm not as smart as God. He's got the big plan, not me.

There have been many experiences with the boys where they were "spreading their wings," and I was terribly frightened that they might die. Each new level of their independence brought me a new and deeper dependence upon the Lord. This was one secret I learned to acquire a deeper faith, letting go of my control, and giving it to God.

Both Sean and Cameron have moved with great strides into the adult world. They have gained many skills. Sometimes they failed and faced painful consequences. Many times they succeeded! Since Cameron is my more neurotypical son, this last chapter will focus more on Sean.

When I think back to that first day of letting Sean ride the little yellow school bus, my heart still skips a beat. I can still see him taking that first big step up to climb into the bus. It was tough, but he managed, and somehow, I did as well.

About a year ago, Sean was having a great deal of anxiety. He wanted to stay another night at our home, but it was Sunday night, and time to go back to his adult family home. We had a routine of bringing him home to visit every other weekend.

That night at his adult family home, around 11:00 p.m., he decided he would sneak out of his home and walk to the bus stop to board the bus and travel to our home. It would normally be about a fifteen-minute bus ride. Unfortunately, his plan would be unsuccessful because he fell asleep halfway to our home. He ended up riding the bus to the end of the line, to the city directly north of us. Now it was midnight, and he was forced off the bus as it was going "out of service" for the night. Sean stepped into the dark night into unknown territory. I don't know how long he walked before calling me.

At that time, we did not have a locator for his phone. We have since wised-up! (We use the Life360 free app.) I ended up calling the police on my landline and kept talking to Sean on my cell phone. It was a completely frustrating experience, not to mention terrifying. He was in a ware-house district.

Except for God answering my prayers, there is no other explanation as to how he finally found a fire station. He told me he rang their doorbell, but no one answered. He saw a low wall, so I told him to jump over and try knocking on a back door. The fire men saw him and just about this same time, the police arrived. They had used technology to "ping" his phone to verify his location.

After the hour of nerve-wracking tension waiting for Sean to be found, I was exhausted. The police questioned him and then questioned me. A social worker was called to assess whether he was being abused and had simply run away. They didn't realize I was the one who wanted to run away! So many sleepless nights with Sean were wearing me down.

After they determined the truth of the matter, my won-derful husband left to go pick him up at 2:00 a.m. After getting him tucked into bed, we all fell asleep exhausted.

I wish I could end the story here, but we have just experienced a similar nightmare. Sean learned how to ride the train recently out of necessity. His new adult family home is a forty-five minute drive away, with no traffic. With Sean attending school in our hometown, we decided that riding the train would be the safest and most efficient manner of transportation.

Very recently, his new caretaker, PJ, called to say that Sean did not depart the train after school. Being a much smarter parent, I quickly looked up his location on my phone by using the Life360 app. In real time, I was watching him speed south on the train. We both suspected that he had fallen asleep. In the end, we would be right.

Now a new dilemma arose. Who do I call: the police, the highway patrol, or the train system? I would end up talking to the police and the train personnel. It is a very confusing and inefficient system for trying to get the train to stop in an emergency.

PJ was a real trooper. He had jumped into his car and was driving parallel to the train by freeway, while Sean's train was zooming south. The train finally went to the end of the line. By this time, Sean had been riding the train for two extra hours. I was nervous that he was medication and food deprived. This is a perfect storm for aggressive behavior.

The story is still a little fuzzy here, but all I know is when PJ found Sean at this final destination, he was acting aggressive with the police. They had handcuffed him. When PJ arrived, they figured Sean would calm down. Wrong! The minute they released the cuffs off his wrists, Sean took off running. For now, his phone was in his backpack with PJ. There was no way of tracking his location!

Sean would be lost in the dark in an unknown city to him for the next two hours. I now felt like I was moving in slow motion. Russ was traveling home from work, and I didn't want to tell him until he was home.

Thankfully, the Lord cleared my thoughts long enough for me to call family and friends for emergency prayer. In between texts, I kept getting calls from the police in the city where Sean was lost and from the police with the train system. It was truly making me more nervous than when this all started.

Just five minutes before Sean was found, I opened my Bible to the Psalms. I have all my favorite uplifting Scriptures highlighted with pink and yellow ink. I started reading them aloud and declaring the goodness of God. I started thanking Him for being in control of this whole situation and for keeping watch over Sean. I was crying the whole time as the reality of his possible death loomed. The police had even asked me if Sean had x-rays of his dental records.

Suddenly, God brought back another time when Sean's possible death loomed large. I gave God complete charge over Sean then as an eight-month-old infant, and I was doing it again now, twenty-five years later.

The ringing phone startled me back into reality. It was Officer Marc. Sean had been found. I was so relieved that I cried with elation! Giving my trust over to Jesus transformed me yet again, strengthening my faith to empower my hope. Where there is hope, nothing is impossible with God!

A Longing Fulfilled

Describe a time when you or someone you love needed protection.

_____

_____

_____

_____

_____

_____

_____

_____

_____

What was your response to that experience?

_____

_____

_____

_____

_____

_____

_____

_____

_____

Find a Scripture that describes how God protects us.

_____

_____

_____

_____

_____

_____

_____

_____

_____

Each time you relive that memory or need protection, start verbalizing your Scripture above.

EPILOGUE

I continue to have difficult challenges with Cameron and Sean. My faith is still being tested and purified. Like me, I hope you have come to realize that no matter how difficult your circumstances are, you can still have hope in your heart.

I still have to work at staying hopeful. But now I'm quicker to give my problems to God. I don't hang on to them like I used to. I have confidence in God to take care of my situation, instead of trying to rely on myself. This requires faith, and the first step is getting to know God through His Son, Jesus. The Holy Spirit will be there to guide and encourage you along your journey.

Once I made the decision to let God be the One I would run to for comfort, guidance, and love, I began to see the bigger picture. I read a poem years ago that helped give me this perspective. It is titled, "The Weaver." It talks about a beautiful tapestry. When we look "up" to try to understand why God has arranged our "tapestry" a certain way, we often see the tangled, confusing mess of threads. We forget that from His heavenly perspective looking down at our lives, God sees the finished tapestry, spun with pure gold, a shimmering masterpiece.

The definition of faith from Hebrews 11:1 is what helped me with this perspective: "Now faith is being sure of what you hope for, and certain of what you do not see." I know God wants to give me a good future, worth hoping for. But for now, I must trust in the here and now, knowing I do not yet always see the manifestation of what I'm hoping for. I have a confident expectation of something good occurring, despite what might be happening at the moment.

One of the most important lessons I learned for keeping hope alive is to remember that I constantly need to feed on the Word of God. The Word is what keeps us nourished and fruitful!

More of my secrets to keeping hope alive are found in the following Supplements section. You will be thrilled with the results when you put the ideas into practice.

Prayer was also vital to developing my faith. As my prayers were answered, my faith grew and so did my hope! I pray that you have come to see that God is your hope, your ever-present help.

A Scripture that has helped keep me strong over the years will bless you too. It's from Romans 15:13, "May the God of hope fill you with all joy and peace as you trust in Him, so that you may overflow with hope by the power of the Holy Spirit."

You have been designed with a heart that longs for eternity, a yearning just for God. He wants to give you the good gifts of joy and peace, but especially hope! He is waiting right now to welcome you home and embrace you with His infinite love.

SUPPLEMENTS

Understanding Hope

Hope is the proper response to the promises of God. It is the confident expectation of something good with faith in God's Word. It is in the future and it is invisible.

To hope is to desire and consider something possible. It is the reason for a longing or desire. It is the desire and search for a future good. It is the possibility of a yearning fulfilled.

As an action, hope is to believe, expect, trust, rely, anticipate, count on, and foresee. As an object, hope is a belief, longing, dream, or desire. It is also an expectation, ambition, assumption, anticipation, or expectancy.

It increases from the power of the Holy Spirit. It is a gift from God. It gives us boldness and strengthens our faith. Hope provides comfort. Jesus is the object of our hope!

Looking at the Hebrew word of hope, we see the word *qavah*. This means a cord (as an attachment) or expectancy. I love the picture that the Hebrew meaning sets up for us. When we trust in the Lord to fulfill a promise, we wait with expectancy. We can picture ourselves literally "tied" to this promise with a cord as we wait with hope!

Please visit me on my website I created just for you at www.sparklinghope.net for weekly blogs on hope, health, and special needs. Visit the Family Room to see more photos from *The Song of My Hope*. Signing up to receive my *Friday Blog* will enable you to download a packet on the secrets to Shalom Health!

Scriptures of Hope

Anxiety. Philippians 4:6–7; Peter 5:7
Confidence. Joshua 1:9; Psalm 37:3; Psalm 57:7; Isaiah 26:3
Contentment. Psalm 107:8–9; Philippians 4:19
Courage. Deuteronomy 31:6; 2 Chronicles 32:7–8; Psalm 27;14; 1 John 5:14
Emotions. Psalm 57:2–3; Psalm 119:50
Faith. Romans 15:13; 2 Corinthians 5:7; Hebrews 11:1,3
Favor. Job 10:12; Psalm 5:12; Psalm 30:7; Hebrews 4:16
Fear. 2 Timothy 1:7; 1 John 4:18
Grace. Luke 2:40; Acts 13:43
Health and Healing. Psalm 30:2; Proverbs 4:20–22; Isaiah 58:8; Jeremiah 30:17; 3 John 2
Help. Psalm 287; Psalm 94:17–19; Nahum 1:7
Holiness. Romans 12:1–2; Ephesians 4:23–24
Hope. Psalm 147:11; Proverbs 13:12; Romans 15:13
Insecurity. Isaiah 41:10; Philippians 4:13
Peace. Psalm 85:8; Isaiah 26:3; John 14:27; Philippians 4:7; 2 Thessalonians 3:16
Power. Isaiah 40:29; 1 Corinthians 15:57; Ephesians 1:17, 19; Ephesians 3:15
Prayer. John 16:24; Hebrews 4:16
Protection. Deuteronomy 33:27; Psalm 32:7; Psalm 52:8–9

Receiving God's Love. John 15:9; Romans 5:5; 1 Corinthians 8:3; Ephesians 3:17–19; Ephesians 4:15; Ephesians 5:2; Jude 20–21

Spiritual Warfare. Romans 8:37

Stress. Psalm 37:5; Isaiah 40:29; Luke 12:27; Philippians 1:10; Philippians 4:6; Philippians 4:8–9; 1 Peter 5:7

Taking Care of Your Body. Proverbs 4:10; Proverbs 4:20–22; Proverbs 16:24; Jeremiah 30:17; 3 John 2

The Goodness of God. Psalm 34:8; Psalm 37:4–6; Psalm 135:3; Psalm 145:9; Jeremiah 33:11; Nahum 1:7; 1 Corinthians 2:9; Philippians 4:19

The Mind. Psalm 139:1–4; Proverbs 3:5–6; Proverbs 23:7; Romans 12:2; Philippians 4:8; 2 Timothy 1:7

The Power of Words. Psalm 19:14; Proverbs 15:23; Proverbs 16:23; Proverbs 25:11; Isaiah 50:4

Trust. 2 Samuel 22:31–33; Psalm 2:2; Psalm 1:2–3; Psalm 62:8; Proverbs 3:5–8; Isaiah 30:15; Hebrews 2:13

Victory. 2 Samuel 8:6; Romans 8:37; 2 Corinthians 2:14

Waiting on God and His Timing. Psalm 145:15–16; Isaiah 30:18; Isaiah 40:31

Walking in Love. Ephesians 5:2; 1 John 4:12

Wisdom. Proverbs 3:5–7; Proverbs 3: 13–15; Proverbs 8:11; Proverbs 8:35

Worship. Psalm 119:38; Ecclesiastes 3:14; John 4:24; Romans 12:1; Hebrews 12:28

Personalizing God's Word

*And the Word of the Lord is flawless, like silver
refined in a furnace of clay, purified seven times.*
—Psalm 12:6

When you see a blank line in the Scriptures below, write in your name. Then read it aloud with your name inserted. This is a powerful tool for renewing your mind with God's Word. You will be amazed how this exercise will infuse you with hope as it transforms you!

"God's way is perfect, His Word flawless. He is a shield; _____ takes refuge in Him. It is God who arms _____ with strength, and makes her to stand on the heights" (Ps 18:30; 32–33).

"_____ praises the Lord who counsels her, at night You instruct her. _____ always sets the Lord before her. Because the Lord is at _____ right hand, she is never shaken. _____ heart is glad and her tongue rejoices; her body also rests secure. The Lord has made known to _____ the path of life; the Lord fills her with joy in His presence, with eternal pleasures at His right hand" (Psalm 16:7–9; 11).

"_____ delight is in the Word of God. She meditates on it day and night. _____ is like a tree planted by streams of water, she is fruitful in season, her leaves never wither. Whatever she does prospers" (Ps 1:2–3).

"_____ lets the Light of the Lord shine upon her. The Lord fills her heart with joy! _____ sleeps in peace because the Lord makes her dwell in safety" (Ps 4:6–8).

"_____ takes refuge in God and therefore is glad. _____ sings for joy! God protects her because she loves Your name and she rejoices in You. You bless _____, she is righteous, You surround her with Your favor as with a shield" (Ps 5:11–12).

"_____ praises the Lord with all her heart. She tells of the Lord's wonders. _____ is glad and rejoices in the Lord, she sings praises to the Lord, O Most High" (Ps 9:1–2).

Secrets for Keeping Hope Alive!

Come with an open heart

- Read the book of Psalms and highlight your favorites.
- Believe and Speak the Word of God.
- Speak a meaningful Scripture through the day, inserting your name to personalize it.
- Cling to the Scripture as though your life depends on it—because it does!
- Sing the Scripture out loud, starting with the Psalms.
- Read a devotional.
- Listen to Christian music.
- Read a Christian magazine article.
- Read books on faith and hope.
- Listen to a sermon on the radio.
- Watch a sermon on the television.
- Join a Bible study that interests you and work on it each day. Sharing with other Christians provide a rich bond.

- Read a meaningful Scripture and ponder it throughout the day asking God to reveal its deeper meaning.
- Buy a journal and write out your sorrows, joys, and thanks to God.
- Memorize a meaningful Scripture once a month.
- Look up a word in Hebrew for a rich reward!

Remember, God desires to spend time with you to show you how much He loves you! He will infuse you with hope as you trust in Him.

Cherished Books

1. *God Meant it for Good* by R.T. Kendall
2. *Health and Wholeness through the Holy Communion* by Joseph Prince
3. *Jesus Calling* by Sarah Young
4. *My Utmost for His Highest* by Oswald Chambers
5. *Praying the Names of Jesus* by Ann Spangler
6. *Praying the Names of God* by Ann Spangler
7. *Secrets of the Vine* by Bruce Wilkinson
8. *Sparkling Gems I* by Rick Renner
9. *Streams in the Desert* by L.B. Cowman
10. *The Power of a Praying Parent* by Stormie Omartian
11. *The Secret Power of Speaking God's Word* by Joyce Meyer
12. *When I Lay My Isaac Down* by Carol Kent

ABOUT THE AUTHOR

Betsy Kay Ridgway, MS, married Russ in 1984 and delayed her career in school counseling to adopt Cameron (now twenty-seven) and Sean (now twenty-six). In 2009, they wove Brent (now thirty-one) into their family.

Betsy has enjoyed leading small groups at church for the past twenty years. For two years, she worked in a Christian high school with students needing academic support. For five years, she helped parents by working as a special education advocate.

After Sean was diagnosed with a brain tumor as a baby, she started researching the brain in hopes of helping him. She also spent years researching the field of special needs. With her overflowing knowledge, she decided to start the Sparkling Hope website to provide hope for families, as well as resources. Her inspiring and educational weekly blogs can be seen at www.sparklinghope.net.

Betsy's unique background and experiences have been woven together to create this book. Her personal stories will inspire you and teach you how to gain hope, despite your challenging hardships.